Saqqara: The History and Legacy of the Ancient Egyptian Necropolis near Memphis

By Sean McLachlan & Charles River Editors

A picture of ruins at Saqqara

About Charles River Editors

Charles River Editors is a boutique digital publishing company, specializing in bringing history back to life with educational and engaging books on a wide range of topics. Keep up to date with our new and free offerings with this 5 second sign up on our weekly mailing list, and visit Our Kindle Author Page to see other recently published Kindle titles.

We make these books for you and always want to know our readers' opinions, so we encourage you to leave reviews and look forward to publishing new and exciting titles each week.

About the Author

Sean McLachlan is an historian and archaeologist who has worked throughout Europe and the Middle East. He has written numerous books and articles on history and is also the author of several works of fiction, including *The Case of the Purloined Pyramid*, a detective novel set in Cairo in 1919. Learn more about his work on his Amazon page and blog.

Introduction

A picture of excavated ruins at Saqqara

Saqqara

Africa may have given rise to the first human beings, and Egypt probably gave rise to the first great civilizations, which continue to fascinate modern societies across the globe nearly 5,000 years later. From the Library and Lighthouse of Alexandria to the Great Pyramid at Giza, the Ancient Egyptians produced several wonders of the world, revolutionized architecture and construction, created some of the world's first systems of mathematics and medicine, and established language and art that spread across the known world. With world-famous leaders like King Tut and Cleopatra, it's no wonder that today's world has so many Egyptologists.

What makes the accomplishments of the Ancient Egyptians all the more remarkable is that Egypt was historically a place of great political turbulence. Its position made it both valuable and vulnerable to tribes across the Mediterranean and the Middle East, and Ancient Egypt had no shortage of its own internecine warfare. Its most famous conquerors would come from Europe, with Alexander the Great laying the groundwork for the Hellenic Ptolemy line and the Romans extinguishing that line after defeating Cleopatra and driving her to suicide.

Perhaps the most intriguing aspect of ancient Egyptian civilization was its inception from the ground up, as the ancient Egyptians had no prior civilization which they could use as a template. In fact, ancient Egypt itself became a template for the civilizations that followed. The Greeks and the Romans were so impressed with Egyptian culture that they often attributed many attributes of their own culture–usually erroneously–to the Egyptians. With that said, some minor elements of ancient Egyptian culture were, indeed, passed on to later civilizations. Egyptian statuary appears to have had an initial influence on the Greek version, and the ancient Egyptian language continued long after the pharaonic period in the form of the Coptic language.

Although the Egyptians may not have passed their civilization directly on to later peoples, the key elements that comprised Egyptian civilization–their religion, early ideas of state, and art and architecture–can be seen in other pre-modern civilizations. For instance, civilizations far separated in time and space–such as China and Mesoamerica–possessed key elements that were similar to those found in ancient Egypt. Indeed, since Egyptian civilization represented some fundamental human concepts, a study of their culture can be useful when trying to understand many other pre-modern cultures.

The pyramids of ancient Egypt have captured the world's imagination for centuries, and while the image that usually comes to mind is of the magnificent pyramids of Giza, there are many other pyramid fields in Egypt, and the one at Saqqara is the oldest and largest. It was the site for pyramids built by at least 11 pharaohs, along with subsidiary pyramids for their queens. In addition to having the most pyramids of any pyramid field in Egypt, Saqqara contains hundreds if not thousands of smaller tombs.

Saqqara is located less than 10 miles south of Cairo on the west bank of the River Nile and runs about 3.75 miles on its north-south axis. The site is generally broken down into the region of North Saqqara and South Saqqara, since there are clusters of monuments on each end, but there are some interesting features in the middle portion as well. While the Step Pyramid of Djoser is by far the most famous monument at the site, Saqqara is a rich network of pyramids, temples, and tombs dating from the first dynasty of Egypt all the way to Greco-Roman times, an impressive span of more than 2,500 years. Indeed, Egyptologists have only uncovered a small fraction of the remains.

Besides the Step Pyramid, several other important discoveries have been made here. Most significant is the earliest example of the Pyramid Texts, found in the pyramid of Unas. Excavations have been continuous for more than 150 years, so dedicated Egyptologists are still uncovering rich tombs, some of them having been undisturbed for more than 2,000 years.

The entire site is a UNESCO World Heritage Site and is open to visitors. While not as grandiose as the pyramids at Giza or as imposing as the temple at Karnak, a visit to Saqqara is well worth the trip, not only to stand on the site of Egypt's first pyramid, but to explore the numerous well-preserved tombs. It is an easy day trip from Cairo, and a full day should be devoted to it in order to fully appreciate the tombs, temples, and pyramids that are open to the public. There is also a museum on site that explains the history of Saqqara and displays some of the artifacts found there.

Saqqara: The History and Legacy of the Ancient Egyptian Necropolis near Memphis examines the history and excavations at the sacred burial site. Along with pictures depicting important people, places, and events, you will learn about Saqqara like never before.

Saqqara: The History and Legacy of the Ancient Egyptian Necropolis near Memphis
About Charles River Editors
About the Author
Introduction
   Note
   Legendary Beginnings
   Djoser and the Step Pyramid
   Other Old Kingdom Monuments
   The Middle Kingdom
   The New Kingdom and the Apis Cult
   The Late Period and the Greco-Roman Period
   Online Resources
   Bibliography
Free Books by Charles River Editors
Discounted Books by Charles River Editors

Note

The absolute dating of individual pharaohs has been a matter of long debate among Egyptologists, mostly due to the existence of several king lists that vary in the number of years they assign to each ruler.

The basic outline comes from Manetho, one of two priestly advisors to Ptolemy I (305-282 BCE). Manetho's *History* divides the pharaohs into 30 native dynasties and gives the number of years each ruler was on the throne, but no complete copy of Manetho's work exists.

Other king lists are also fragmentary. The Palermo Stone from Dynasty V (2498-2345 BCE) is a fairly complete list starting from the last Predynastic kings, but it sadly ends in the middle of Dynasty V. The Royal List of Karnak goes all the way to Tuthmosis III (1504-1450 BCE) and is especially useful in that it records many of the minor rulers of the Second Intermediate Period, when Egypt was divided into two or more states. The Royal List of Abydos skips these kings but runs all the way to the reign of Seti I (1291-1278 BCE). The Royal Canon of Turin is a badly damaged papyrus dating to around 1200 BCE that gives the precise length of reign of each ruler, often down to the day. Many portions of the list are missing, however.

Discoveries of other texts and radiocarbon dating have helped refine the dates, but there are still competing theories regarding the chronology, and all have both merits and problems. For the sake of consistency, this work uses the chronology set forth by Egyptologist Peter A. Clayton in his various works. The reader should note that while Clayton's chronology is a popular one, it is by no means universally accepted.

Legendary Beginnings

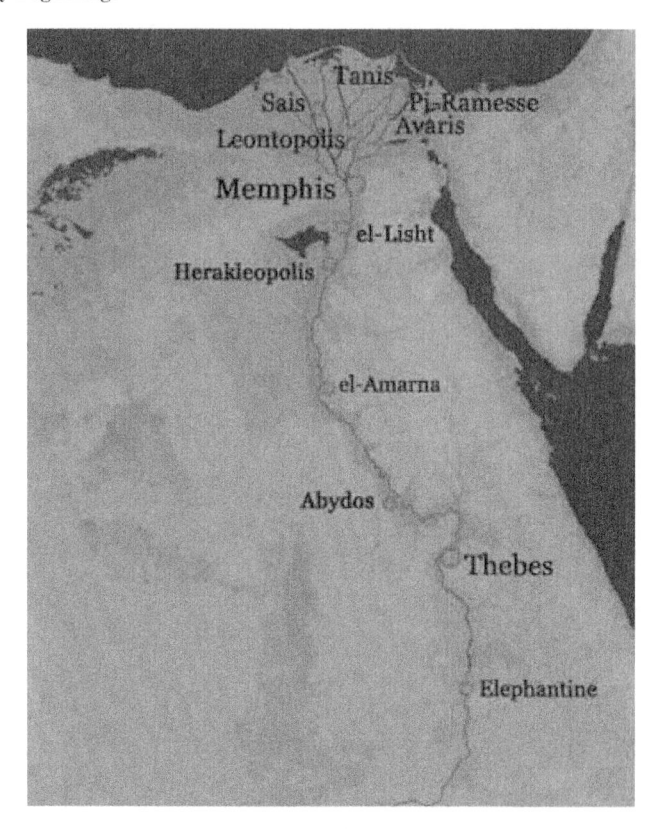

A map of Ancient Egypt

According to tradition, the Ancient Egyptian city known now as Memphis was founded in the year 2925 BCE by the pharaoh Menes. Legend has it that Menes, believed to be the first pharaoh of Egypt's first dynasty, established his capital at Memphis by diverting the Nile River with dikes. Menes is also credited as being the first of Egypt's pharaohs to unite Egypt in a single, centralized monarchy. A 3rd century BCE Egyptian historian referred to this legendary pharaoh as Menes, but the 5th century Greek historian Herodotus gave his name as Min, and in the Ancient Egyptian native-king lists of the 19th dynasty, his name is listed as Meni.

A series of excavations at Saqqara have found that the earliest royal tomb built there belonged to the pharaoh Aha, but Mantheo referred to Menes as a Thinite and monuments to the pharaohs

Narmer and Aha have been found at Abydos, a Thinite royal cemetery. Furthermore, archaeologists have unearthed a slate palette which features the image of Narmer wearing the white and red crowns of Upper and Lower Egypt, which suggests that it was Narmer who was responsible for Egypt's unification.

Today, scholars have begun to speculate that the legendary pharaoh tradition knows as Menes was actually one of three archaic Egyptian pharaohs: Scorpian, Narmer, or Aha. Some have come to believe that the unification process took place over the reigns of several pharaohs and that Menes is simply a representation of all the pharaohs who were involved. According to Mantheo, however, the pharaoh Menes reigned for a full 62 years before he was at last carried off and killed by a hippopotamus.

Pictures of excavations at Saqqara

Though the identification of Menes continues to prove difficult, it is clear that the first dynasty's rise to power was marked by an uptick in wealth. This is apparent from an increase in source materials such as inscriptions on stone vessels, ivory and wood labels, and seal impressions. These finds confirm that the first dynasty oversaw significant changes to the country's administration, namely the unprecedented expansion of the power of the central government. The available sources also testify to the construction of palaces and the founding of royal estates, as well as the naming of high-ranking government officials by which these processes were overseen.

A picture of the Memphis statue known as the "Berlin Green Head"

An inscription on a necropolis at Saqqara that depicts Ankh-ef-en-Sekhmet, his wife Hathor-em-hat, and their daughter, with close-cropped hair, kneeling at center. The three are entertained by a harpist named Psamtik-seneb, who "plays the harp for the good of their spirits everyday." The harpist's name means "may King Psamtik be healthy."

Not surprisingly, the pharaohs of the first dynasty (~3000-2800 BCE) were fond of making demonstrations of their absolute power, but they did so in some unusual ways. During this period, it was apparently not uncommon for royal servants and some members of the royal elite to be killed or buried alive when the pharaoh's tomb was sealed, as they were expected to continue serving their ruler eternally in the afterlife.

One label, dated to the reign of Aha, provides record of a military campaign undertaken against the land of Ta-Seti (Nubia). Given the abundance of stone vessels from Syria-Palestine that may be dated to this period, the pharaohs of the first dynasty also had begun to participate in extensive trade with some of their neighbors. From these artifacts and contemporaneous inscriptions, it is even possible also to determine the names of Egypt's first rulers: Narmer, Aha, Djer, Djet, Den, Anedjib, Semerkhet, and Qa'a.

There is evidence to suggest that Memphis underwent a period of turmoil after the 33 year reign of Qa'a. Two further first dynasty pharaohs after Qa'a - Ba and Seneferka - have been attested to in some (but by no means all) inscriptions dating back to this period. Furthermore, the name of the first pharaoh of Egypt's second dynasty, Hotepsekhemwi, translates to "the two powerful ones are at peace," which may be interpreted to mean that Hotepsekhemwi once again reunited the warring factions of Upper and Lower Egypt. The fact that several names of second dynasty pharaohs are mentioned only in the records of Upper or Lower Egypt also attests to the idea that Egypt was once again divided into two kingdoms for at least part of this period.

The archaeological record suggests that the second dynasty consisted of approximately seven pharaohs—Hotepsekhemwi, Nebre, Ninetjer, Weng-sekhemwi, Peribsen, Sekhemib Perenmaat, and Khasekhemwi—and lasted for approximately 150 years, from 2800-2650 BCE. The name of the last pharaoh of the second dynasty, Khasekhemwi, seems to have modeled his name after Hotepekhemwi's. Khasekhemwi means "the two lords are at peace within him," which suggests that Khasekhemwi had once again managed to reunite a divided Egypt, and the fact that Khasekhemwi's name was the first name since Ninetjer's to be found throughout the entirety of Egypt seems to affirm this.

It was also during this second dynasty that the pharaohs of Ancient Egypt officially moved their royal cemetery from Umm el-Qu'ab in Middle Egypt to Saqqara near Memphis. Egyptologists are certain that this significant change in tradition carried important religious, political, and historic consequences, but the lack of archaeological work makes it nearly impossible to determine what exactly these consequences were. That said, the relocation of the royal cemetery at the beginning of the second dynasty indicates the rising preeminence of Memphis during what has come to be known as the Early Dynastic Period.

At some point towards the end of Early Dynastic Period, the rulers of Ancient Egypt permanently took up residence at a fortress called "Ineb-Hedj" (The White Walls), named after its magnificent fortifications, but the city of Memphis itself has proven nearly impossible to excavate. The remains of this once sprawling city have come to be scattered, and urban development and the cultivation of the region's fertile fields preclude any real possibility of extensive excavation.

It is perhaps a testament to the difficulty of Memphite excavations that the legendary white walls of the royal residence at Memphis were not unearthed until 21st century. In 2015, a team of Russian archaeologists working near Saqqara happened upon several fragments of white limestone, which they believed once formed the walls of the ancient capital. Along with these fragments of limestone, the team also discovered some well-preserved bronze and stone artifacts. It is hoped that this incredible find will shed some light upon the history of this fascinatingly enigmatic ancient city.

By the end of the Early Dynastic Period, the city had officially come to be known as Memphis, one of many major changes to have taken place during this era. At this point, Ptah was officially recognized as the god who was both patron and protector of the royal city, as well as the patron god of artisans and craftsmen. In some contexts, Ptah was also considered to be the creator god.

According to a document called the Memphite Theology, the god Ptah created humans through the power of his speech and heart. Indeed, the Memphite Theology introduced the concept of man having been shaped in the heart of a divine creator god and created through his divine utterance. This text is unique among Egyptian creation texts, as it gives an abstract account of the creative act where all other texts give a physical analogy. The Memphite Theology is also evidence of the philosophical sophistication of Memphite priests.

With the potential exception of the royal residence, the Great Temple to Ptah at Memphis was the largest, most prominent, and most important structure within the city of Memphis. The Great Temple to Ptah, allegedly also founded by the great Menes, occupied a large precinct in the middle of the great city. Though restricted to all except priests and pharaohs, the Great Temple to Ptah was nevertheless regarded as one of the foremost places of worship in Ancient Egypt, and some believe that it was even larger than the Great Temple to Amun at Karnak. If this is true, the Great Temple to Ptah would have been the largest place of worship ever constructed. Though a team of archaeologists working in the early 20th century once unearthed several sections of the Great Temple to Ptah, they left the remains they discovered exposed, and they were soon lost to the depredations of nearby villagers.

Pictures of the ruins of the temple

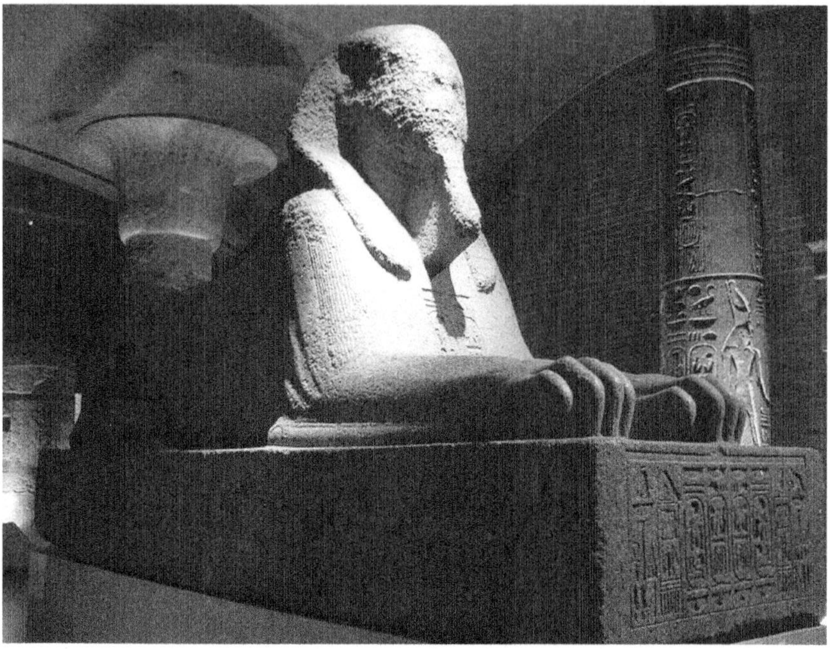

A sphinx of Ramesses the Great located in the temple

Since excavating the actual city of Memphis has proven excessively difficult, the vast majority of information about the golden age of Memphis comes from excavations of its nearby royal necropolises. As it turns out, the way in which the rulers of Old Kingdom Memphis prepared for their deaths provides an abundance of information about what was going on while they lived. This is, of course, a frustratingly indirect way of piecing together the history of the great city, but there can be no doubt that the rich archaeological legacy discovered at the sites of the Memphite necropolises provides at least some consolation for the near-silent record of "living" Memphis.

As such, some of the best evidence for Memphis' rise to preeminence comes from the royal tombs which were first built at Saqqara by the pharaohs of the second dynasty. It is at Saqqara, for example, that archaeologists have discovered two suites of subterranean rock-cut chambers and galleries, which they have associated with the pharaohs Hotepsekhemwi and Nynetjer. Each of these subterranean suites had an astonishing storage capacity (4,000 square meters in the case of Hotepsekhemwi) in order to ensure that the tomb could hold the full wealth of the deceased pharaoh. These second dynasty tombs were significantly more intricate than their first dynasty counterparts, which had consisted of little more than a series of pits dug into the ground. In contrast, the tombs of the second dynasty pharaohs were comprised of long, subterranean corridors with plenty of storage rooms on either side to ensure that the pharaoh interred within would not be without any of his wealth and treasure in the afterlife.

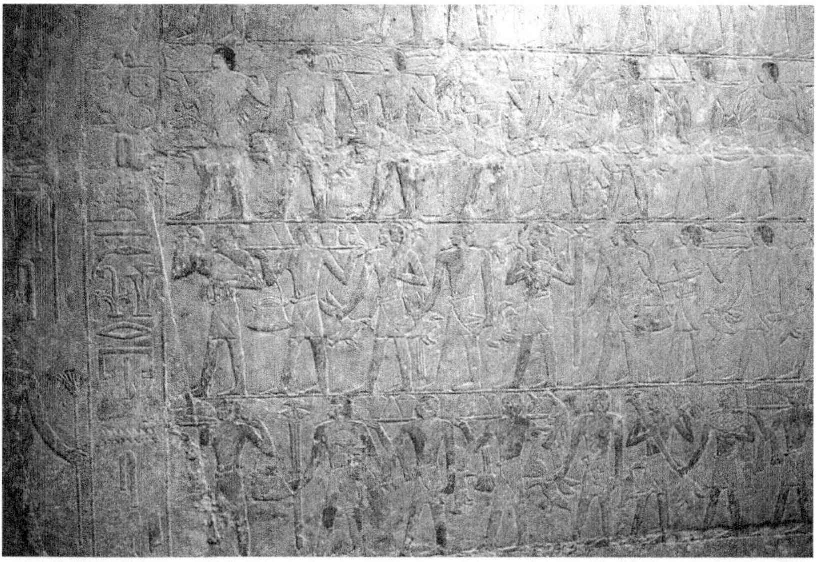

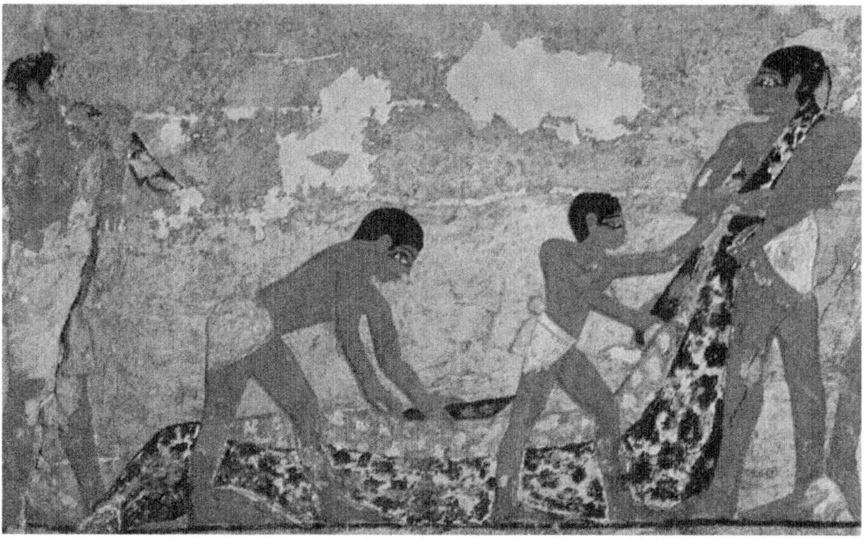

Pictures of inscriptions and art found in pharaohs' tombs in Saqqara

The western half of Memphis is quite close to Saqqara. From the city, the Egyptians could walk past a now vanished lake and up a long sloping wadi to the Saqqara plateau. To one side of this wadi rises a high cliff, and on the edge of this cliff are a string of Dynasty I tombs called *mastabas*. A mastaba is a rectangular structure generally a few meters high. The term is actually the Arabic word for "bench" because it resembles the solid rectangular benches Egyptian farmers make outside their front doors to this day. Some of the larger mastabas at Saqqara are 150 meters (492 ft.) long and 50 meters (164 ft.) wide. The exteriors had niched facades made to resemble buildings. This was a popular architectural style with alternating recessed and projecting sections that made the walls look like the crenellations on top of medieval castles, but set on their side. The recessed panels were painted yellow to make them look like wood, while the forward, broader faces had various patterns that resemble woven mats. Surrounding some of the mastabas were cow heads made of clay and fixed with real horns.

The interiors of the mastabas can be quite complex. They are generally a series of rooms, the center ones interconnecting and containing the burial, while smaller rooms acted as storage for goods used in the afterlife. These storage rooms tended to be sealed off from one another and had to have been filled before the mastaba was completed. One supposes this was partially to deter tomb robbers but as with the vast majority of ancient Egyptian tombs, the mastabas were looted in antiquity.

Some mastabas had a vaulted tumulus over the burial chamber. Another had a stepped tumulus over the burial chamber, anticipating the later Step Pyramid of Djoser. Some mastabas had descending stairs that cut into the bedrock beneath the mastabas and allowed for more chambers. These subterranean chambers would become common in later mastabas and pyramids.

A mastaba

It has long been a matter of debate whether these mastabas are the tombs of nobility or of Dynasty I pharaohs. Several Saqqara mastabas contain seals and other items with the names of pharaohs and queens, but they also contain similar material with the names of the nobility. Over in Abydos, the homeland of the earliest dynasty, are a series of large pit graves with smaller graves of retainers arranged around them. Most scholars now believe that the pit graves at Abydos are the actual Dynasty I royal tombs, while those at Saqqara are for the nobility, and the royal names found within the Saqqara mastabas are in fact the rulers of the deceased. Anyone who had such an elaborate tomb would have been a member of the social elite and would have had close ties to the government.

Royal burials and more noble burials began to appear in Saqqara during Dynasty II (2890-2686 BCE). One is the purported tomb of Hotepsekhemwy (c. 2890-??? BCE), founder of Dynasty II. Not much is known about the pharaoh, not even the length of his reign, which most Egyptologists estimate to be about 25-29 years. The official name of this tomb is Gallery Tomb B, located beneath the later Unas necropolis. It is assigned to Hotepsekhemwy because many seal impressions bearing his name were found in the long, narrow underground gallery. On the other hand, several seal impressions of Hotepsekhemwy's successor Raneb were also found there, leading some investigators to assert that it was actually Raneb's tomb. Whatever the case, it's unlikely that it was used for both men, as this was not normal practice at any time in Egypt.

Raneb's successor Nynetjer, whose reign also lacks precise dates, is definitely buried at Saqqara. He had a large gallery tomb beneath the necropolis of Unas measuring 106 by 94 meters (348 x 308 ft.). Like Gallery Tomb B, a long ramp leads down to a warren of rooms and passages. While it had been looted in antiquity, the tomb still contained large numbers of knives and jars for wine and beer. Oddly, markings on some of the wine jars show they had been reused from tombs of late Dynasty I. Alabaster bottles were also found, as well as traces of later intrusive burials from the New Kingdom. It was not unusual for tombs to be reused in later periods when the family of the original owner had died out.

The last pharaoh of Dynasty II, Khasekhemwy (?-2686 BCE), chose to be buried at the traditional site of Abydos, but he also built a grand mortuary enclosure at Saqqara. Called the Gisr el-Mudir, it measured 650 by 350 meters (2,133 by 1,148 ft.). The limestone wall, while crudely made, is impressively thick, being in reality two walls 15 meters (49 ft.) apart and the space in between filled with gravel, crushed stone, and sand. At its highest point it stands up to 5 meters (16 ft.) but originally probably reached twice that height.

One of the few things known about Khasekhemwy's reign is that he put down several rebellions to reassert the unity of Egypt, which had fallen into peril. Thus, the fact he was buried at Abydos in Upper Egypt but built substantially at Saqqara in Lower Egypt may have been a symbolic way to demonstrate his rule over both portions of the country.

Egyptologists have long argued over the purpose of the enclosure of Gisr el-Mudir, since no buildings have been found within it. There is some evidence of a small building in the northwest corner, where a fair amount of rubble was found, but it is unclear if these ruins dated to a later period or were even the remains of a building at all. Some researchers say Gisr el-Mudir was never completed beyond the walls, which do appear to have been finished, while others claim that open-air ceremonies took place inside and no buildings were ever intended.

By the end of Dynasty II, Saqqara was established as the center for royal burials, and during the following dynasty, Saqqara became the launching point for a new era of Egyptian history with the development of the first pyramids.

Djoser and the Step Pyramid

The rulers of Dynasty III (2686-2613 BCE) greatly expanded their activity at Saqqara. It is unclear where the first pharaoh of the dynasty, Sanakhte (2686-2668 BCE), was buried, but the second king of the dynasty, Djoser (2668-2649 BCE), chose Saqqara. Both rulers had active reigns, putting down rebellions and expanding their territory. It appears Djoser pushed as far south as Aswan and the First Cataract, which would be the southern border of Egypt for centuries to come, although some rulers moved even further south.

Saqqara was already established as a burial ground for Memphis, but Djoser and his architect Imhotep would turn it into something far grander. They decided to build the tomb in stone rather than mudbrick, and on a truly vast scale. There was nothing in previous Egyptian architecture that even came close to their achievement.

The origins of the pyramids, including their chosen shape and design, stretch all the way back to the mythological stories of the ancient Egyptians. As a culture, the Egyptians are known for their obsession with death, so it is ironic that these lavish tombs were inspired instead by a story of creation – the story of birth.[1] In Egyptian mythology, the world was formed from out of the depths of a primal ocean that was both infinite and bereft of life, and these ancient waters parted when the sun rose for the very first time. This origin was something that the Egyptians referred to as the "first occasion". The chaotic waters of the lifeless ocean, an entity that they called Nu, parted as a pyramid shaped mound rose up through the waves. This shape, the benben, was the first part of Earth, the first sign of life, rising from out of the waters. The mythological imagery of Egypt naturally reflected the reality of their environment, where the rising waters of the Nile flooded the land, only to recede again and leave fertile ground with rich muds ready to be seeded with crops, the source of Egypt's bounty and life.[2]

While the shape of the pyramid derives from mythology, the Egyptians had several reasons for building them. The pyramids served religious and funerary purposes, while also serving as reinforcing power structures for Egypt's rulers, but the process of building also served a valuable practical function. Egypt required a large work force to produce the food needed to feed its people, as the rich soils surrounding the Nile needed to be seeded, crops tended and harvests reaped. For one entire season out of the year, however, the farming belt of Egypt was covered by water as the Nile flooded its banks, leading to a large part of Egypt's population being idle during that time. The building of monuments was a valuable method of keeping an otherwise idle population active, thereby guaranteeing employment for all throughout the year. Farmers in the Old Kingdom period who were idle and wanted to work during the Nile's period of inundation could get paid and avoid taxes by working on pyramid building projects. Egyptian citizens with nothing to occupy them while their farming lands were under water could thus spend the season

---

[1] Rosenberg, Donna. 1986. *World Mythology.* HARRAP, Great Britain. pp 166-177.
[2] Leeming, David Adams. 2010. *Creation Myths of the World.* AB.C.-CLIO, Santa Barbaro. pp 102.

erecting timeless monuments to their ruler, receiving wine and beer thrice daily as part of their working conditions.[3]

Given the difficult and no doubt deadly nature of the labor, it has long been assumed that the Egyptians wouldn't have resorted to building the pyramids all by themselves. Popular culture images of present day have shown erroneous depictions of Jewish slaves being whipped as they dutifully push vast blocks of sandstone along on trundling wooden logs. Such was the case in *The Ten Commandments*[4] and the animated *Prince of Egypt* even showed wooden scaffolding around the Sphinx.[5] In reality, wood was a rare commodity in Egypt, imported from abroad and used as a prestige item. The Sudan supplied ebony wood, pine and cedar were imported from Syria,[6] and large timbers were imported from Lebanon for shipbuilding.[7] The lack of wood in the largely desert regions of Egypt led fringe theorist Erich von Daniken to conclude that aliens must have been behind the construction of these great edifices, an explanation that has since had its own impact in popular culture through television programs like *Doctor Who*[8], as well as film and television franchises like *Stargate*.[9] "The stone blocks used for building," von Daniken stated, "were moved on rollers. In other words, wooden rollers! But the Egyptians would scarcely have felled and turned into rollers the few trees, mainly palms, that then (as now) grew in Egypt, because the dates from the palms were urgently needed for food and the trunks and fronds were the only things giving shade to the dried up ground. But they must have been wooden rollers, otherwise there would not even be the feeblest technical explanation of the building of the pyramids."[10]

Von Daniken's central argument about the achievements of the past is that humans did not have the capacity to attain such successes and were therefore not responsible for the great monuments of antiquity. He suggested instead a utopian past when space travelers, possibly native Martians seeking to escape changing environmental condition on their own world, escaped to Earth and brought a wealth of knowledge and technology along with them.[11] Von Daniken theorized that "a group of Martian giants perhaps escaped to Earth to found the new culture of homo sapiens by breeding with the semi-intelligent beings living there… giants who come from the stars, who could move enormous blocks of stone, who instructed men in arts still

---

[3] Seawright, Caroline. 2013. *Egypt: The Nile Inundation*. Site accessed 4 September 2013. http://www.touregypt.net/featurestories/nile.htm
[4] DeMille, Cecil B (director). 1956. *The Ten Commandments*. Paramount Pictures, USA.
[5] Chapman, Brenda; Hickner, Steve; Wells, Simon (directors). 1998. *The Prince of Egypt*. Dreamworks Pictures, USA.
[6] Egyptian Government. 2013. *Egypt: Trees in Egypt*. Site accessed 4 September 2013. http://www.touregypt.net/featurestories/trees.htm
[7] Brier, Bob. 2007. How to Build a Pyramid. In: Archaeological Institute of America. 2007. *Archaeology Volume 60 Number 3, May/June 2007*. Archaeological Institute of America, USA.
[8] Russell, Paddy (director). 1975. *Doctor Who: Pyramids of Mars*. BB.C., UK.
[9] Emmerich, Roland (director). 1994. *Stargate*. Canal, USA.
[10] von Daniken, Erich. 1972. *Chariots of the Gods? Was God an Astronaut?* Gorgi, Great Britain. pp 97.
[11] von Daniken, Erich. 1972. *Chariots of the Gods? Was God an Astronaut?* Gorgi, Great Britain. pp 99.

unknown on Earth and who finally died out."[12]

However, experimental archaeology has come about as a profession to try to figure out the feasibility of these kinds of building projects by using reconstructive approaches that used the known building conditions and experiences of the past. Archaeological experiments found that while wood was in short supply, one thing that Egypt had plenty of during the time of the Nile inundation was mud. Using mud bricks to shape mud ramps, it was possible for limestone blocks to be pushed and hauled along the slippery surface of the wet ramps. Such experiments have even been used to estimate the building period times for pyramid construction. Although not conclusive in proving the methods of the past, they certainly demonstrate the possibilities that past Egyptian craftsmen could have used.[13] Another theory is that the process of building was split between an inner and outer ramp. While the outer ramp was removed, the inner ramp became part of the pyramid's structure.[14]

The tradition of pyramid building was a long one in ancient Egypt occurring over hundreds of years, with techniques developing and improving, only to be forgotten and lost again. As a result, even as subsequent generations contributed new large-scale construction programs that changed the face of Egypt, they did so in quite different manners. The first of these was the Step Pyramid, located in the northwest of the city of Memphis in the Saqqara necropolis of Egypt. Today it is known as the Step Pyramid due to its stepped appearance, but in Egyptian times it was referred to as kbhw-ntrw. Commissioned by and made for the burial of the Pharaoh Djoser, its design and construction was overseen by his vizier Imhotep. The name Imhotep has since become infused with popular culture through the popular series of Mummy movies, where the mummified remains of Imhotep are reanimated through the power of an ancient curse, leading to the shambling, linen-wrapped and decomposing undead monster haunting the hapless treasure seekers who dared disturb his resting place.[15] In reality, the ancient Imhotep was a talented architect and builder who succeeded in creating something that had never been seen before. It was a design that would often be repeated, even improved upon, and it gave birth to an ancient industry dedicated to the afterlife, one that would leave an indelible mark on Egyptian life as well as death.

---

[12] von Daniken, Erich. 1972. *Chariots of the Gods? Was God an Astronaut?* Gorgi, Great Britain. pp 155.
[13] Lehner, Mark. 1997. *The Complete Pyramids*. Thames and Hudson, Slovenia.
[14] Brier, Bob. 2007. How to Build a Pyramid. In: Archaeological Institute of America. 2007. *Archaeology Volume 60 Number 3, May/June 2007*. Archaeological Institute of America, USA.
[15] Sommers, Stephen. 1999. *The Mummy*. Universal Pictures, USA.

The Step Pyramid, also known as the Pyramid of Djoser

**A relief inside the tomb of the Step Pyramid depicts Djoser facing the temple of Horus.
Photo by Juan R. Lazaro**

Imhotep took a number of roles in his life. He was the high priest of an ancient Egyptian sun cult, chief counselor to the Pharaoh, an accomplished sculptor and an architect. He improved upon the existing funerary design of the mastaba by building mastabas of dwindling size each on top of the other. When it was finished, he had produced a stairway to heaven upon which the Pharaoh Djoser could ascend into the next life.[16]

The Step Pyramid was crafted using cut stone construction, with the large steps decreasing in size as they rose in height, and the pyramid originally reached a total height of approximately 200 feet. Although currently appearing in the natural colors of the worn materials used in its construction, the pyramid was originally clad in limestone that was polished bright white, thus shining like a beacon under the bright light of Egypt's sun. Around it, a mortuary complex was built with various decorated structures for ceremony and religious rituals.[17]

---

[16] Time Life Books. 1987. *The Age of God-Kings*. Time Life Books Inc, Amsterdam. pp 60.

Temples near the Step Pyramid

While it now looks old and has been surpassed by the pyramids that came after it, it is important to remember that at the time of its construction, the Step Pyramid was not only brand new but unlike anything Egyptians had ever seen. The Step Pyramid was radically different from the preexisting architecture of Egypt, as were the techniques used to make it. While mud brick had previously been used for building practices, this cut stone edifice was much more labor intensive. It would also prove to have much greater longevity as a result. For centuries, the Step Pyramid dominated the landscape in which it was situated, due not only to its imposing size but also the shining white exterior that made it stand out all the more.

The exact date of construction for the Step Pyramid is not known, but Djoser was estimated to have reigned for approximately 19 years between 2667-2648 BCE. The name Djoser is a modern one attributed to him, much as the Step Pyramid has been named long after the fact. In his tomb, he is referred to by his Horus name Netjerykhet.[18] Ruling during Egypt's Third Dynasty, Djoser sought to align himself with eternity through the building of this structure. His ambitious plan for a monument to mark his burial, so expertly realized by his advisor and architect Imhotep, set the stage for the tradition of pyramid building that followed.

---

[17] Time Life Books. 1987. *The Age of God-Kings*. Time Life Books Inc, Amsterdam. Pp 62-63.
[18] Wilkinson, Toby. 2000. Royal Annals of Ancient Egypt. Routledge, USA. pp 79 & 258.

Djoser's burial vault was made of dressed granite laid in four courses, but the tomb was robbed during the ancient world, so by the time it was excavated in modern times, the body had long ago been removed. Undeterred, French architect Jean-Phillipe Lauer chose not just to excavate the area but also to reconstruct key portions of the 15-hectare sized complex surrounding the Step Pyramid.[19]

Reconstructed corridor leading to the entrance of the Step Pyramid

---

[19] Lauer, Jean-Phillipe. 1961. *The Pyramids of Sakkarah (Les Pyramides De Sakkarah)*. Imprimerie De L'Institut Graphique Egyptien, France.

Djoser and the Construction of the Stepped Pyramid

Djoser seems to have taken his inspiration from the Gisr el-Mudir in order to make a large funerary enclosure around his pyramid. This would become a standard but not universal practice for later pyramids.

The Step Pyramid is not a true pyramid in that it has a square base. Instead, it is rectangular, like the mastabas from which it evolved. Its base measures 121 by 109 meters (397 by 358 ft.) and rises in six steps to 60 meters (197 ft.) in height. Extensive analysis of the construction shows that it originally started out as a large mastaba, and then Imhotep and Djoser changed their minds and put a series of smaller mastabas on top of the original to turn it into a stepped pyramid. Even this did not satisfy them and they later expanded the pyramid to make it wider and taller.

The substructure beneath the Stepped Pyramid is highly complex, more so than most later pyramids. A series of staircases, chambers, and passageways surround a large burial chamber. Because of structural weakness, this underground network has not been completely explored. The passageways spread out like fingers around the main burial chamber and dead end. These were doubtless filled with grave goods and bear little or no decoration, except for one section inlaid with blue faience tiles that features three false doors depicting Djoser. Scholars believe this portion was made to represent the king's palace. The builders left it unfinished, however, with one wall still rough and some of the decoration showing signs of having been put up in haste.

The burial vault is accessed by a vertical shaft 7 meters (23 ft.) square and 28 meters (92 ft.) deep. This shaft is a little off from the center of the completed Stepped Pyramid and only reaches the top of the initial mastaba. When it was decided to expand the mastaba into a pyramid, this shaft got filled in and a long staircase cut into the side of the pyramid. This entrance, too, was blocked when the builders decided to make the pyramid even bigger, and a third and final access had to be cut via a trench to the north.

The burial vault itself changed over time. It originally had alabaster walls and a floor of diorite or schist. The ceiling was made of limestone blocks with five-pointed stars carved in bas-relief. This is the first example of a starry roof in an Egyptian tomb, the idea being that the spirit was able to fly out into the universe. These stones were then shifted around to nearby locations when the burial vault was redone.

The final burial vault design measures 2.96 x 1.65 meters (9.7 x 5.4 ft.) and is 1.65 meters high and is made of granite. The roof is a series of rectangular granite stone blocks with a granite plug at one end that measured one meter in diameter, two meters in height, and weighed 3.5 tons. It blocked off a hole in the roof through which the body must have been moved into its final resting place. After this was accomplished, the hole was plugged and the entire access way filled in with stones. All this was to no avail; the tomb was fully plundered and Djoser's mortal remains have vanished.

On the eastern edge of the original mastaba are 11 vertical shafts containing some human remains as well as about 40,000 stone vessels, mostly plates and cups made of fine alabaster. Some bore names, but not of Djoser. The remains of one female have been radiocarbon dated and turned out to be several generations older than Djoser. Some scholars theorize that earlier tombs were plundered and their contents moved here so Djoser could enjoy his eternal rest with his ancestors.

An extensive mortuary complex surrounds the Step Pyramid, establishing a tradition that would continue for all later pyramids, and despite being the first, it is also one of the largest and most elaborate mortuary complexes of any Egyptian ruler. The entire complex is surrounded by a limestone wall 10.5 meters (34 ft.) high in a niched pattern. The wall runs 1,645 meters (5,397 ft.) to enclose a rectangular area of 15 hectares (37 acres) and was surrounded by a moat (although this name is somewhat misleading since it was not filled with water). The entrance was on the east wall.

Much of the enclosure to the south of the Step Pyramid is taken up by a large courtyard surrounded by several buildings, some of which were functional and others were false buildings. The functional buildings would have been where the various rituals took place, while the false buildings were used by Djoser's *ka*, or life force. The southeast portion of the enclosure has a narrow courtyard meant for the Sed festival, the king's jubilee festival of renewal that included rituals to ensure his physical and supernatural renewal. Its appearance here was apparently to show that Djoser remained fit to rule even after his death. The buildings flanking this courtyard are false chapels and are stone forms of earlier style buildings that had been made of wood and reeds. The ones to the east have the slim pillars and arched roofs of the canonical shrine of Lower Egypt, and those to the west resemble the blockier shrines of Upper Egypt. The hieroglyphs for both of these shrines closely resemble the actual buildings and together symbolize Djoser's perpetual right to rule over a unified Egypt.

Along the southern edge of the enclosure is the South Tomb, an enigmatic subterranean complex. It is similar to the substructure of the Stepped Pyramid itself in that there is a long descending staircase, a central shaft leading to a burial chamber, and a scaled-down version of the network of tunnels. One tunnel is even decorated like the king's palace, just like the one below the Stepped Pyramid. On one of the false doors in this section is a bas-relief of Djoser running as part of his proof of fitness in the Sed festival, while holding a legal deed of ownership for all of Egypt. About halfway down the staircase is a side corridor filled with jars. On top of them lay the remains of a wooden stretcher, box, and posts similar to those used to carry statues.

The burial chamber is too small for a body and sarcophagus, being only 1.6 meters (5.2 ft.) square and 1.3 meters (4.3 ft.) high, but otherwise it is similar to the real burial chamber, right down to the granite plug in the ceiling. The interior is stained green from a copper lining that has since disappeared.

Nothing was found within and there are various theories as to the South Tomb's purpose. Some believe it was for the *ka*, while others theorize that the burial vault once contained the royal crowns or perhaps Djoser's internal organs. If it was for the *ka*, then it is a precursor to the cult pyramids found at later royal mortuary complexes.

Beyond the Sed Court lies the House of the South and the House of the North, representing the traditional shrines at Hierakonpolis and Buto. The House of the South (Upper Egypt) has pillars with capitals shaped like lilies, one of the symbols of the region, and the House of the North (Lower Egypt) has pillars with capitals in the shape of papyrus. These were, like those chapels around the Sed Court, false buildings in which no religious ritual was performed.

The mortuary temple was built against the Step Pyramid's north face. In later pyramids, it would be moved to the east.

The entire building project was the responsibility of Imhotep, and his work was so celebrated that he would be revered in later generations and raised to the status of a god. His cult flourished at Saqqara for centuries.

Djoser was the first Egyptian pharaoh to have taken on any kind of a monumental building project whatsoever, let alone a project of such unprecedented scope and nature, so the logistical problems that would have arisen in such a construction project would have been equally unprecedented. Suddenly, materials, supplies, and men had to be transported to Saqqara from all over Egypt, and once there, the thousands of men that would have been needed to work on such a large project required not only food and housing but training as well, since most had no experience whatsoever working with the material Djoser wanted them to use. Thus almost overnight Egypt saw the creation of a class of men whose sole purpose was to be able to handle such large and complicated problems. These men would have been able to apply the same kind of managerial knowledge to other projects of similar scale, such as organizing a large trading expedition or planning the invasion of a foreign nation.

The political benefits of such a monumental building project cannot be overstated. Upon its completion, Djoser's pyramid complex was, of course, an effective piece of propaganda, attesting to the stone-like permanence of the central government over a united Upper and Lower Egypt. At the same time, it was actually the process of building the complex that really solidified this message, because few things are more threatening than idle hands to an already tenuous political situation, and Djoser would have surely recognized the potential danger of having hundreds of thousands of farmers with plenty of extra time on their hands while the Nile was in its annual period of flooding. Commissioning the labor of these men for a pyramid project guaranteed that these men would be too busy to have time getting caught up in things like political unrest. Furthermore, it put men from all over Egypt on the governmental payroll, ensuring that the entire nation was equally dependent on the central government. So long as the pyramid industry was successful, the central government knew that it would not have to worry anymore about the threat of civil unrest.

Other Old Kingdom Monuments

The landscape of Egypt was forever altered by the design of the Step Pyramid, and the rulers who followed Djoser were keen to put their own stamp on the landscape by proceeding with similar examples of monumental architecture. The next attempt occurred during the reign of the Pharaoh Sekhemkhet Djoserty. The second ruler of Egypt's Third Dynasty, Sekhemkhet Djoserty was Djoser's direct successor and has been estimated as ruling Egypt for approximately 6 years, with his own pyramid constructed sometime around 2645 BCE.[20]

The Pyramid of Sekhemkhet was of a grand design, located to the southwest of the Step Pyramid. Everything about its design suggests that the monument was envisaged to build upon the example of the first pyramid and surpass it both in scale and style. But unfortunately, possibly due to his period of reign being shorter to Djoser's, the Pyramid of Sekhemkhet was never actually completed. Far from dwarfing the Step Pyramid, the unfinished masterpiece instead barely progressed above ground level, earning it a less flattering nickname in the years to come: the Buried Pyramid. The fact that the Buried Pyramid literally did not get off the ground meant that it was not even discovered until the middle of the 20th century.

---

[20] Gardiner, Alan H. 1997. *The Royal Canon of Turin*. Griffith Institute, Oxford, UK.

The unfinished Pyramid of Sekhemkhet

The Buried Pyramid lay unnoticed until 1951, when Egyptologist Zakaria Goneim spotted a rectangular rise on the ground a few hundred meters to the southwest of the Step Pyramid. Irregularities in the ground often signal that there is an archaeological feature beneath, and a visitor to any of the large Egyptian sites will see several intriguing lumps and hills. The problem is that until they are excavated, it is difficult to know if they are features of interest or rubbish spoils from previous excavations, and sometimes simple sand dunes can look irritatingly like archaeological features until someone starts digging into them. Another problem is that sites like Saqqara are so vast that many features have never been investigated for lack of time and manpower.

What Goneim found when he excavated was the base of a step pyramid that had only been completed up to its first course. The pyramid measures 120 m (394 ft.) to a side and calculations extrapolating from the existing base indicate it would have been 70 meters (230 ft.) tall with seven steps if finished, making it taller than Djoser's pyramid. Sadly, it ended up only reaching 7 meters (23 ft.). The pyramid was surrounded by an enclosure wall 5.18 m (17 ft.) high and 18.28 m (60 ft.) thick. The enclosure wall encompassed a large area, measuring 518 m (1,700 ft.) on the north-south axis and 182.8 m (600 ft.) on the east-west axis.

The enclosure wall had many niches and false doors, and in one spot the name Imhotep is inscribed. This hints that the same architect who built the Step Pyramid of Djoser might have worked on this one. Imhotep may have wanted to outdo himself.

On the north side of the unfinished pyramid is a descending passage leading to the tomb beneath the pyramid. This had been completed and used, so it appears that the pyramid was halted after the pharaoh died, a fate that befell many pyramids and tombs. The tomb was mostly plundered in antiquity, but numerous artifacts had been left behind, including papyri, stone vessels, and bones from animal offerings. The tomb robbers also missed a wooden casket filled with gold jewelry, cosmetic cases, beads, and several jars with the name of the pharaoh on them.

Behind a blocked wall was an undecorated chamber with a large alabaster sarcophagus sealed with mortar. Unfortunately, the sarcophagus turned out to be empty. Goneim was clear in his report that the sarcophagus had not been broken into, so why it was empty is a mystery.

There is also an unusual U-shaped subterranean corridor that goes around the northern side of the pyramid, but beneath it, and it reaches a little more than halfway along the west and east sides. It contains a row of 136 unfinished galleries. Whether these would have contained statues, burials, or treasure is unknown, but it appears they were never stocked.

In 1963, a second tomb to the south of the first one was discovered, similar to the South Tomb of Djoser's mortuary complex. In it was a wooden coffin with the remains of a 2-year-old child and some fragments of gold leaf. This child was perhaps the son or daughter of Sekhemkhet. It could not be of Sekhemkhet himself since he ruled for six years and a relief in the Sinai shows him as an adult.

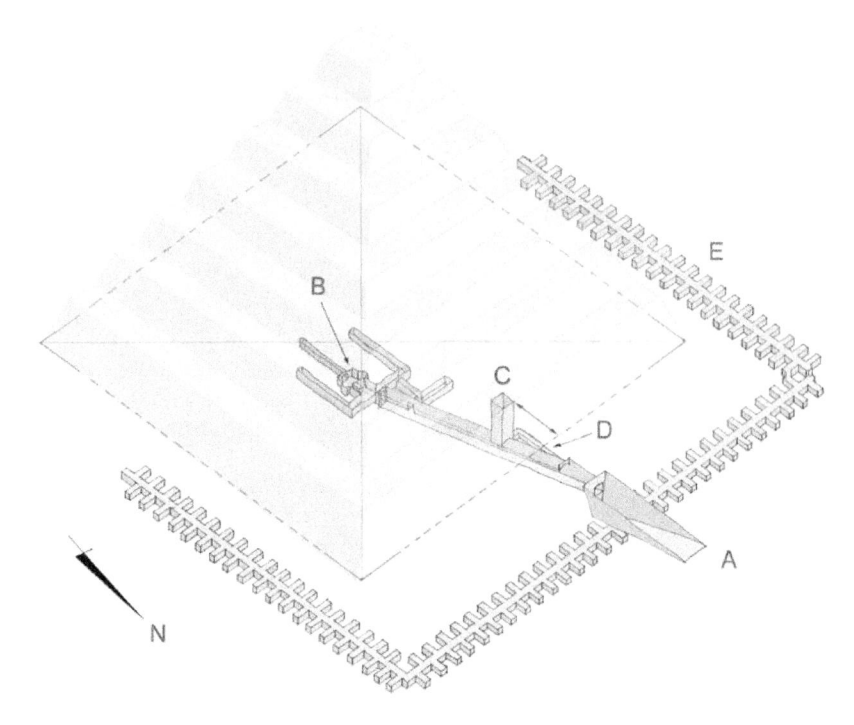

Franck Monnier's picture of a computer generation depicting the intended design for the Buried Pyramid.

The pharaohs of Dynasty IV chose to build their pyramids elsewhere, most notably at Abusir, Giza, and Dashur. The exception to this was the last pharaoh of Dynasty IV, Shepseskaf (2504-2500 BCE), who not only chose to return to Saqqara but built himself an old-style mastaba instead of a pyramid. Shepseskaf was the son of Menkaure (2532-2504 BCE), who built the third pyramid at Giza, and while it is smaller than those of Khufu and Khafre, it is still a grand monument, which makes it all the stranger his son chose a relatively modest resting place. While historians have tried to explain these odd decisions, no one has come up with a reason for Shepseskaf turning his back on the Dynasty IV pyramid fields or for building himself a mastaba.

With that said, it is indeed a large one, measuring 96.6 by 74.4 meters (317 by 244 ft.) with a slope of 70°. Its lowest course was red granite, while the rest of the casing was high quality limestone. The entrance is on the north side, with a sloping passageway leading to a series of chambers, the westernmost being the burial chamber, which contained fragments of the sarcophagus. A small mortuary temple on the eastern side had a false door for the deceased's spirit, an offering hall and storage rooms, as well as an inner and outer courtyard. Both the mastaba and mortuary temple are surrounded by two mudbrick walls. The causeway and valley tomb for this mastaba survive but have not been excavated.

While Shepseskaf departed from tradition in many ways, he did continue the tradition found at Giza of having a stone causeway leading from the tomb to the valley, where a temple was situated. It was at this valley tomb where a ship bearing the body was docked, and, after the proper rituals were completed in the valley temple, the body was brought up the causeway to its final resting place. Saqqara is too far from the Nile for this kind of arrangement, but the annual flooding of the Nile left a series of lakes in the low valleys nearby, so the causeways of Shepseskaf's mastaba and the later Saqqara pyramids led down to valley temples on the shores of these lakes.

No queen's tombs have been found around Shepseskaf's mastaba, an unusual omission for which there is no good explanation. Moreover, the choice of location is interesting because Shepseskaf chose to place his mastaba in South Saqqara, where there were no prior royal burials. It remained the southernmost royal tomb for the entire site.

Shepseskaf also finished his father's mortuary temple at Giza, although in a rather slapdash fashion with mudbrick rather than stone. Given that fact, it's possible that the extravagant spending in Dynasty IV had left the government either without the funds or the will to create giant monuments.

That changed with the next dynasty, although pyramid building would never again reach the heights it had at Giza. The first ruler of Dynasty V, Userkaf (2498-2491 BCE), continued the tradition of being buried at Saqqara and built a pyramid there a little outside the northeast corner of Djoser's enclosure. Like the pharaohs who had preceded him, he sought to reinforce existing power structures and ensure his memory by commissioning a series of monumental works. This included a large mortuary complex consisting of a mortuary temple, an offering chapel and a cult pyramid. It also included his own pyramid, as well as a separate pyramid and mortuary temple for his wife, Queen Neferhetepes.

The pyramid complex of Userkaf was built around 2490 BCE in the pyramid field at Saqqara. It was built directly to the northeast of the Step Pyramid, which had been commissioned by the Pharaoh Djoser so many centuries earlier, but unlike the Step Pyramid, the style of the pyramids located within the complex followed the general design of their immediate predecessors. Constructed from dressed stone with cores made up from rubble, the pyramids were situated in a complex of larger size, using different architecture and locations for the interior compared to those that had most recently come before it. In a sense, the Saqqara location was both new and old, as it brought pyramid construction back to the site of the Step Pyramid, a place that had not been used for pyramid complexes since.[21]

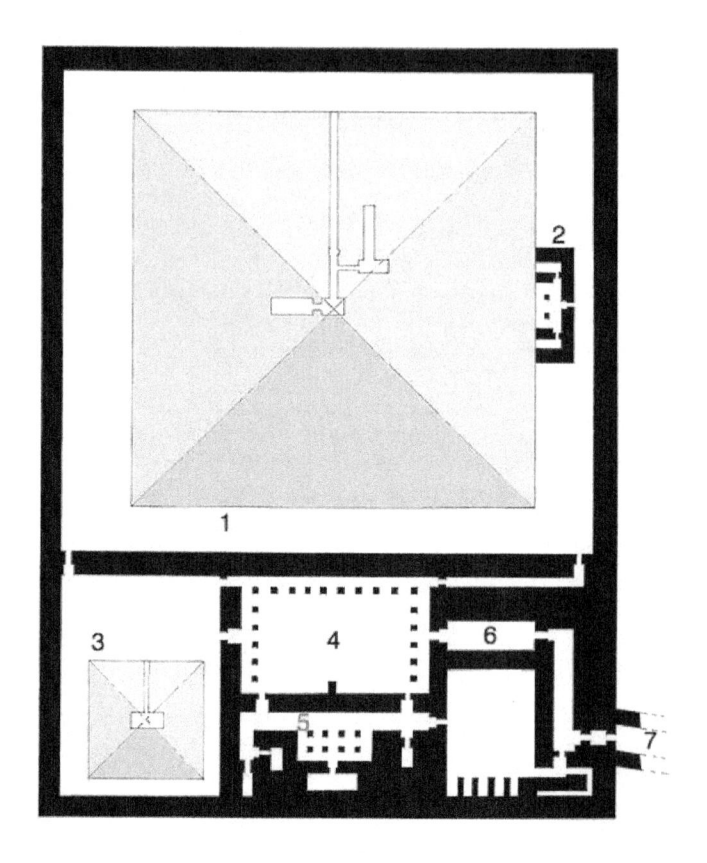

The pyramid complex: 1) Main pyramid, 2) Offering Hall, 3) Cult pyramid, 4) Courtyard, 5) Chapel, 6) Entrance corridors and 7) Causeway. Photo by Iry Hor

The main pyramid of Userkaf reached a height of nearly 175 feet, with a base of over 200 feet following its completion. Like the Great Pyramid of Giza, the sides of the pyramid ascended upward at an angle of 53 degrees, and roughly hewn blocks of local limestone were used to build up a step-like rubble core for the center of the pyramid. A rubble core meant less work during the construction phase, but as the outer shell was cannibalized for other projects and the high quality Tura limestone was taken, the inner core was exposed to weathering and erosion. Thus, during the reign of Ramesses II, some 1,500 years after the construction of the pyramid complex of

---

[21] Shaw, Ian (ed). 2000. *The Oxford History of Ancient Egypt*. Oxford University Press, UK. pp 480.

Userkaf, it underwent some restoration works. The complex was also used during the Saite period as a cemetery, sometime between 664 and 525 BCE.

The ongoing removal of the limestone exterior meant that the rough rubble interior continued to degrade over time, and the main pyramid of Userkaf was eventually left in ruins. Today, there is little left to mark its existence apart from a conical hill in the pyramid field at Saqqara. The pyramid came to be known locally as El-Haram el-Maharbish ("Heap of Stone") due to its dilapidated state of repair. The pyramid of the queen was likewise ruined by the same process, leaving its funerary chamber exposed and leaving the once grand pyramid resembling nothing more than a mound of rubble.[22]

The ruins of the pyramid of Neferhetepes

Excavation was undertaken at the complex by a variety of archaeologists, from Orazio Marucchi as early as 1831, through to John Shae Perring and Richard Lepsius. Identification of the commissioning pharaoh was determined when a colossal red granite head of Userkaf was identified in the archaeological deposit at the site.[23] Despite a grand design and intentions toward

---

[22] Lehner, Mark. 1997. *The Complete Pyramids*. Thames and Hudson, Slovenia.
[23] El-Khouly, Alky. 1976. Excavation at the pyramid of Userkaf: preliminary report. In: Egyptian Exploration Society. 1978. *The Journal of Egyptian Archaeology. Volume 64.* pp 35–43.

longevity, the pyramid complex of Userkaf is a lesson about the effects of time and the ravages of those that follow, with the impressive pyramids of the past ultimately reduced to rubble and sand.

The dilapidated pyramid of Userkaf with the Step Pyramid in the background

Userkaf was a major patron of the sun cult, and in the layout of his mortuary area he changed the location of his mortuary temple from the east of the pyramid—where they were usually located for previous pyramids—to the south. Some Egyptologists theorize this was so the temple would catch the sun's rays all day long.

In the same vein, religious texts from the period show an increased emphasis on sun worship related to the honoring of a deceased pharaoh. Offerings would go through a ritual of consecration at a sun temple before being offered to the dead pharaoh at the mortuary temple. Other scholars give a more mundane reason for the unusual placement of the temple, saying that a moat ran around Djoser's complex and thus there was no room for the mortuary temple to be built in the traditional place.

The mortuary temple, although in a poor state of preservation, must have been grand. A massive granite head of the pharaoh was found there, and it is calculated that the entire statue would have stood 5 meters (16 ft.) tall. Fragments of relief from the walls are of high quality and show boats going through swamps of papyrus reeds.

While a few sculpture fragments survive from this mortuary complex, little else remains and the pyramid is too ruined to enter. The exterior was removed at some time in the past for use in later construction, leaving the vulnerable core to erode and collapse until it became the rather unassuming heap it is today, but its proximity to the mortuary complex of Djoser, who was revered in ancient times, must have added to its luster.

Also unlike the large pyramids at Giza, Userkaf's pyramid does not have internal chambers. Rather, the burial chambers were first dug into the bedrock, roofed over, and the pyramid built on top. The entrance is from the pavement on the north side of the pyramid, rather than on the side of the pyramid itself as was common in pyramids of the previous dynasty. The entrance passage slopes down, heading south under the pyramid for 18.5 meters (61 ft.). Two portcullises of red granite blocked the hallway to keep out tomb robbers, although like with the other pyramids this effort was in vain. At the end of the tunnel was a small network of rooms for Userkaf's burial and grave goods. Little was found except for a chest that once contained the canopic jars that once held the pharaoh's internal organs, and fragments of the basalt sarcophagus.

At the southwest corner of Userkaf's mortuary complex is a small cult pyramid. These are a common feature next to pyramids and appear never to have been intended to house a burial. Just what they were for is a matter of debate. Many believe they housed the pharaoh's *ka*, his spirit or vital essence. The cult pyramid once stood 15 meters (49 ft.) high, 21 meters (69 ft.) to a side, and had a 53° angle. Usually the cult pyramid is to the southeast of the main pyramid, but in in the unusual layout of Userkaf's mortuary complex it is to the southwest. It is in a poor state of repair and little remains today.

A smaller mortuary complex for his queen Neferhetepes stands 10 meters (33 ft.) to the south of Userkaf's mortuary complex. This pyramid was quarried so extensively for stone that its inner chambers have been revealed. Nevertheless, enough remains to calculate that it once stood around 17 meters (56 ft.) tall and 26.25 meters (86.1 ft.) to a side, with an angle of 52°. A small mortuary temple stood to the east but is in poor condition. There is no evidence of a cult pyramid but considering how much the entire site had been removed for later building, it may have disappeared entirely.

Records show that Prince Khaemweset, one of the sons of Ramesses II (1279-1212 BCE), restored the pyramid complex of Userkaf, but by the Third Intermediate Period it had fallen into disrepair, and the temples were partially dismantled. During Dynasty XXVI (664-525 BCE), it became a cemetery. In fact, one large shaft tomb cut right through Userkaf's mortuary temple.

The next pyramid to be built at Saqqara has only recently been identified. Just to the northeast of the pyramid of Teti (see below) stands a pyramid that was extensively quarried in later years, so much so that it has been dubbed the Headless Pyramid. Egyptologists were divided over whether this was the resting place of the Dynasty V king Menkauhor (2422-2414 BCE) or the later king Merikare of Dynasty X (c.2050 BCE). It wasn't until excavations in 2008 by famous Egyptian researcher Zahi Hawass revealed a substructure typical of Dynasty V pyramids. No inscriptions were found but now most scholars believe the pyramid to be that of Menkauhor. No other Dynasty V pharaohs had an unidentified pyramid so it stands to reason that Hawass's hypothesis is correct.

The pyramid measures 52 meters (171 ft.) to a side but is too fragmentary to determine its original height or angle. The substructure had been looted in antiquity and little other than a broken sarcophagus lid was found. Its ancient name, which we know from texts found elsewhere, was "The Divine Places of Menkauhor."

Menkauhor's successor, Djedkare-Isesi (2414-2375 BCE), built a pyramid on a high spur at the southern edge of the Saqqara plateau that is now little more than a heap of rubble resembling a large sand dune. Originally it stood 52 meters high (170.6 ft.), measured 78.75 meters (258.4 ft.) to a side, and had an inclination of 52°. Its ancient name was "Beautiful is Isesi."

The burial chamber was guarded by three large portcullises blocking the entrance passage but robbers circumvented these, stole the burial goods, and stripped the burial chamber of its decorated lining blocks. The black basalt sarcophagus was smashed. A mummy was found amid the ruins, presumably that of the pharaoh himself. The man was aged about 50, indicating that Djedkare-Isesi had still been in his teens when he ascended the throne.

The pyramid had an associated mortuary temple, cult pyramid, and queen's pyramid with its own mortuary temple and cult pyramid, all in a poor state but offering up a few tantalizing finds including high quality reliefs and statuary. One interesting feature are the pylons flanking the entryway to the complex. This is an innovation that would see common use in later construction, most notably in famous temples such as Karnak.

The queen's mortuary complex stands to the northeast of Djedkare-Isesi's. Sadly, there is no record of the name of the queen buried here. The associated valley temple has not been excavated.

Djedkare-Isesi's mortuary complex broke new ground at Saqqara, as it was the first pyramid to be built south of the main area a full 2 km (1.25 miles) south of Djoser's mortuary complex. Djedkare-Isesi chose a prominent place to be buried, atop a piece of high ground that at that time had no surrounding monuments. Even today his pyramid remains quite visible, and local villagers call it "the Sentinel."

The pyramid of Djedkare-Isesi

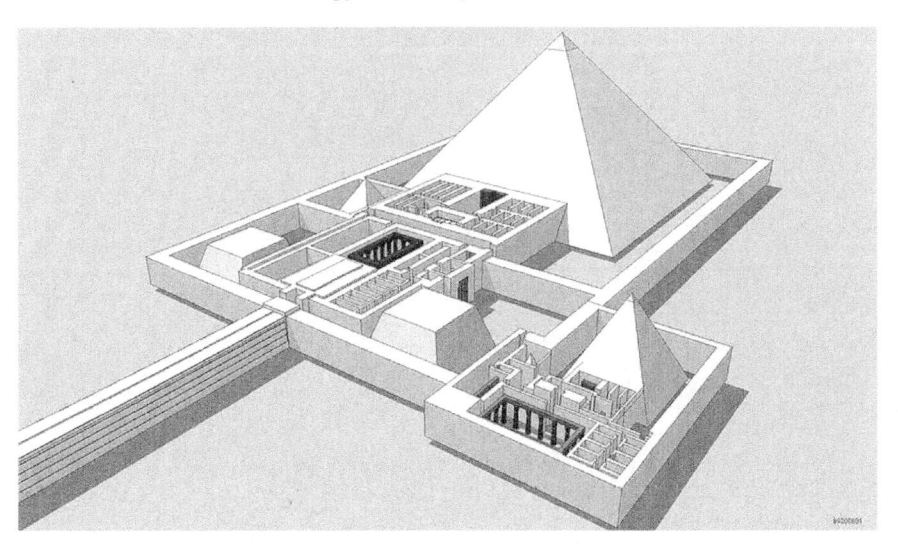

Computer generated layout of the complex

The issue of tomb robbing by this time was evidenced in the design of this pyramid structure. It incorporated three large portcullis slabs as countermeasures to such robbery.[24] There is even documentary evidence recorded of these ancient thieves, such as one stating, "[W]e went to rob the tombs in accordance with our regular habit and we found the pyramid of King Sekemre-shedtawy. We took our copper tools and we broke into this pyramid through its innermost part. Then we broke through the rubble and found the pharaoh lying at the back of his burial place. The noble mummy was completely bedecked with gold, and his coffins were adorned with gold and silver inside and out and inlaid with all sorts of precious stones."[25] The punishment of this historic confessor is not on record, but punishments were known to be severe, including the mutilation of noses and ears. Sometimes, the guilty party was placed on a stake.[26]

Even with harsh penalties for those caught, and the countermeasures Pharaoh Djedkare-Isesi added to his burial chamber, it all inevitably proved unsuccessful. By the time archaeologists came to examine the pyramid, its burial chamber had long ago been plundered.

The most important of the many Dynasty V monuments at North Saqqara is the pyramid of Unas (2375-2345 BCE), the last ruler of the dynasty. This complex is just southwest of Djoser's enclosure, and it is the first pyramid to be decorated inside with extensive hieroglyphic inscriptions. These were the so-called Pyramid Texts.

---

[24] Brown, Dale (ed). 1992. *Egypt: Land of the Pharaohs*. Time Life Books, Virginia, USA. pp 20.
[25] Brown, Dale (ed). 1992. *Egypt: Land of the Pharaohs*. Time Life Books, Virginia, USA. pp 21.
[26] Brown, Dale (ed). 1992. *Egypt: Land of the Pharaohs*. Time Life Books, Virginia, USA. pp 21.

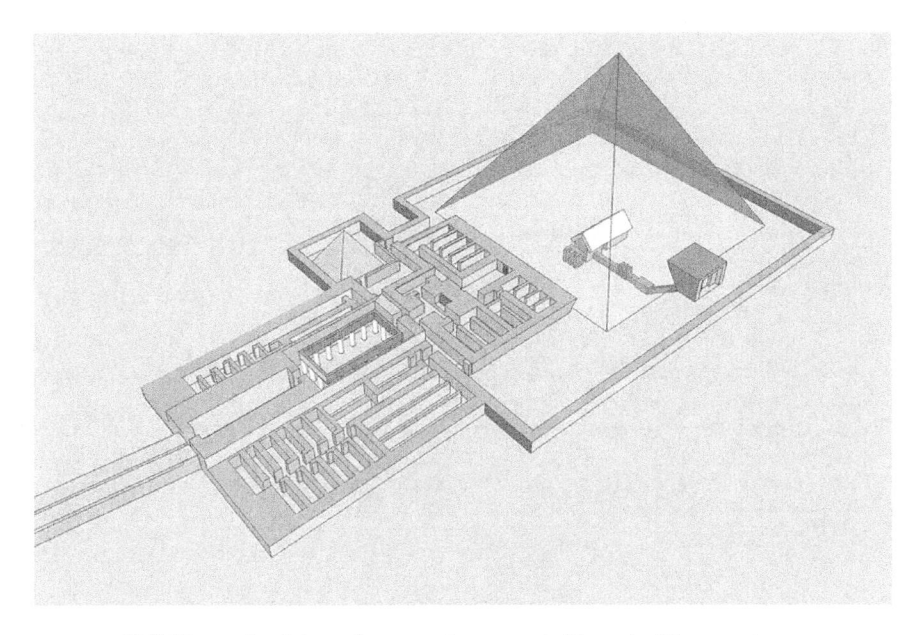

R.F. Morgan's picture of a computer generated layout of the complex

As builders had done for many years, Unas's construction crew liberally borrowed material from the nearest pyramid neighbor: Djoser's Step Pyramid. Furthermore, material from his complex was put to use in a new context by plugging holes and gaps in the wadi located immediately adjacent to Unas's causeway. Ironically (and at least somewhat fittingly), the same kind of masonry plundering eventually took place on Unas's pyramid as well, exposing the core and leading to its inevitable deterioration. Today, the once grand pyramid has been so severely weathered that it now looks more like a natural hill feature than a pyramid structure. The burial chamber was also plundered long ago, but when excavations took place, archaeologists found it still contained some remnants, including a skull, right arm and shin. Whether or not these body parts once belonged to Unas is uncertain.[27]

---

[27] Lehner, Mark. 1997. *The Complete Pyramids*. Thames and Hudson, Slovenia.

The pyramid of Unas

Pyramid Texts in Unas's funerary chamber

The pyramid was originally 43 meters (141 ft.) high and 57.75 meters (189 ft.) to a side, with a 56°18'35" angle. Its ancient name was "Perfect are the Places of Unas." As with previous pyramids of this dynasty, it had a rubble core that became exposed when the exterior dressed stone was carted away. Some of the exterior stones have survived in situ, and an inscription on the south side tells how the pyramid was restored in Dynasty XIX by Khaemwaset, the High Priest of Memphis and son of Ramesses II.

Also in the burial chamber were the partial remains of a male mummy, presumably that of Unas although there is no proof of this. The pharaoh's consorts are buried in a series of mastabas to the northeast of the pyramid.

The mortuary temple is nearly identical in layout to that of Djedkare-Isesi in that it has an entrance hall and then a columned hall flanked by storage rooms. Beyond this lay the inner temple with niches for statues and a sanctuary. It continued the innovation of pylons, although not on such a grand scale as Djedkare-Isesi's temple.

The causeway linking the Pyramid of Unas to the water is well-preserved and part of it has been restored to its original height, making it one of the more interesting features for modern visitors. It was roofed over except for a slit in the center to allow light in. The lively painted bas-reliefs show sailing ships, marketplaces, hunting scenes, and grim portrayals of a famine that apparently occurred during Unas' reign. The valley temple had a complex floor plan and graceful granite columns with capitals in the shape of palm fronds.

To the south of the causeway are two stone-lined boat pits similar to those next to the Pyramid of Khufu at Giza. Unlike the examples at Giza, no boats were found in these pits and it is unclear if they were ever used or perhaps acted merely as symbols.

While the exterior of the pyramid is somewhat unimpressive, it has one of the most archaeologically important interiors in all of Egypt. The burial chamber walls are covered in long vertical hieroglyphic inscriptions. Taken together, they are called the Pyramid Texts and include 283 different spells to help the soul make it to the land of the dead. The soul was required to prove its worthiness and respond correctly to a series of monstrous guardians before having its heart judged to see if the soul was worthy of making it to the next world. Some of these spells were apparently recited at various points during the burial ceremony. This in turn led to the Coffin Texts being developed later in the Middle Kingdom Period, and then the Book of the Dead from the New Kingdom era to the Ptolemaic Period.[28] This notion of magic inscriptions also played a part much later in history through pop culture's fixation on the idea that the pharaohs' mummies had curses. The idea that grave robbers and archaeologists suffered from these kinds of curses remains popular even today.[29]

Unas did not have an heir, so there was a brief period of political unrest before the founding of Dynasty VI. Once the situation stabilized, the pharaohs continued to build pyramids in North Saqqara, and they continued the Pyramid Text tradition, using many of the spells found in the Pyramid of Unas and adding new ones, until there were a total of 400 spells (though none of the pyramids used all 400 spells).

Subsequent pyramids were not as large or grand as their predecessors, and in many cases they have not stood the test of time as well. The Pyramid of Teti, ironically named Teti's Places Are Enduring, is one of these.

The first ruler of Dynasty VI, Teti (2345-2333 BCE) hailed from Memphis and thus continued the tradition of using Saqqara as the royal burial ground. He managed to reunite Egypt and added to his legitimacy by marrying one of Unas's daughters. His pyramid stands on the northern edge of the Saqqara plateau and is the northernmost pyramid at the site. It measures 52.5 meters (172.2 ft.) high, 78.75 meters (258 ft.) to a side, and has an angle of 53° 7' 48".

Like previous ones, it had a rubble core that now lies exposed, making the pyramid look like an inglorious heap. Passing through the entrance via a chapel by the northern face, however, the

---

[28] Lehner, Mark. 1997. *The Complete Pyramids*. Thames and Hudson, Slovenia.
[29] Sommers, Stephen. 1999. *The Mummy*. Universal Pictures, USA.

visitor is treated an antechamber and vaulted burial chamber filled with Pyramid Texts, a ceiling covered in engraved stars, and a basalt coffin missing its lid. Some grave goods remained until modern times, including stone mace heads and one of Teti's canopic jars. More gripping is the plaster death mask of Teti himself, giving us a unique look at the face of an Old Kingdom pharaoh. The wooden interior coffin was also found and is now on display in the Cairo Museum.

The pyramid of Teti

Text inscriptions found in the burial chamber

The sarcophagus of Teti. Photo by Jon Bodsworth

Little of the mortuary complex to the east of the pyramid has survived, aside from fragments of the mortuary temple to the east and a cult pyramid to the southeast with its own (empty) chamber beneath it. The reason for this is that in the Late Period a temple to Anubis was built on the site, erasing much of the earlier construction except for the basic layout of the foundations. Both the causeway and the valley temple have disappeared.

To the north of Teti's pyramid are the pyramids of his queens Iput and Kawit. Iput's pyramid still contained her cedar coffin and skeleton.

Teti's reign had to deal with powerful nobles in the capital and the provinces, and to stabilize his rule, he married one of his daughters to a noble named Mereruka, who also became his vizier. This mastaba is the largest of the non-royal tombs at the site, with 32 rooms. It is one of the best preserved in all of Egypt and has some breathtaking interior decoration, with extensive bas-reliefs that have preserved much of their original color. Scenes include hunting, fishing, playing board games, and standard depictions of servants bringing offerings to the deceased. The depictions of nature scenes are especially well done. One shows a hippopotamus giving birth, only to have the baby emerge from its mother straight into the jaws of a waiting crocodile. The false door at the offering hall through which the *ka* passes in order to receive the offerings is decorated with a painted statue of Mereruka carved almost in the round. Mereruka's royal wife and his son were also interred in the mastaba.

Teti's successor, Pepi I (2332-2283 BCE), also had an extensive mortuary complex at Saqqara, this time in the southern part of the site. The pyramid, another rubble-filled structure that has fallen into ruin now that the casing has been taken, once measured 52.5 meters (172.2 ft.) high and 78.75 meters (258.4 ft.) to a side with an angle of 53° 7' 48", precisely the same angle as Teti's pyramid. Today, the mound only stands 12 meters (39.4 ft.) high and has a bowl carved out of the center by grave robbers. Its ancient name was "The Perfection of Pepi is Established," which in ancient Egyptian is Men-nefer Pepi. This name was later corrupted by Classical writers and applied to the city, which is why it's now known as Memphis.

The interior chambers were accessed by an entrance to the north. They contained portions of the Pyramid Texts, as did some of the five pyramids for Pepi's queens located to the south of the main pyramid.

Pepi's burial chamber preserved large sections of the Pyramid Texts, and its ceiling is covered with carved stars. Pepi's shattered sarcophagus remains inside, inscribed with a line from the Pyramid Texts. Researchers also found a canopic chest of pink granite in a niche set in the floor, the four canopic jars containing the organs of the pharaoh.

Pepi's pyramid had a large mortuary temple to the east laid out in the typical plan of his predecessors. Its limestone blocks have mostly disappeared, but the floor plan is clear enough. Some statues of bound prisoners were uncovered, but it is unclear where in the temple they originally stood.

Part of the causeway has survived, linking it to a valley temple that has not been excavated. Many valley temples have been lost due to the shifting of the river and centuries of agricultural activity. A cult pyramid stood to the southeast of the main pyramid, with a ramp on the north face leading to a chamber beneath.

Pepi reigned for 50 years and built extensively all across Egypt. His successor, Merenre (2283-2278 BCE), only lasted five years on the throne and did not have time to leave much of a mark on history. He did, however, serve as co-regent for several years in his father's old age. Both men expanded into Nubia and sent extensive trading expeditions abroad.

Merenre's pyramid at South Saqqara has the exact same dimensions as Pepi's, dimensions that would become standard. This pyramid was known in ancient times as "The Perfection of Merenre Appears". The interior had a standard layout, being entered from the north and the access passageway protected by three heavy stone portcullises.

The black basalt sarcophagus in the burial chamber is mostly intact, although it was found open. A mummy of an adult male was found inside and was for some time assumed to be that of Merenre himself, but it is now generally believed to be that of a Dynasty XVIII individual. Such intrusive burials were common practice in ancient times, and generally occurred many centuries after the initial burial when the authorities were less concerned over the sanctity of the tomb's original occupant. Like in Pepi's burial chamber, there was a niche in the floor for the canopic chest, but none was found. Passages from the Pyramid Texts lined the interior of the pyramid, with the spells and layout of these writings being quite similar to that of Pepi's pyramid.

The mortuary temple appears never to have been completed, perhaps due to the pharaoh's short reign. This sad fate frequently befell pharaohs who died suddenly or who were unpopular with their successors. Pyramid complexes were so expensive that the reigning king often had few resources with which to honor his predecessor.

The next king was Pepi II (2278-2184 BCE), who had the longest reign of any pharaoh. He apparently was only 6 when he came to the throne, and he lived to a ripe old age. His mortuary complex was placed on the southernmost point of Saqqara near the mastaba of Shepseskaf. The pyramid has identical dimensions to his predecessors, and its ancient name is "Pepi is Established and Living." The interior arrangement follows familiar patterns, and the black granite sarcophagus is still inside.

The mortuary complex is laid out in a standard fashion, with a mortuary temple to the east, a cult pyramid to the southeast, and three queens pyramids to the south and northwest. Unusually, the valley temple has also survived.

Fragments of the mortuary temple decoration show Pepi II defeating the enemies of Egypt, some of them in animal form. One shows the king killing a Libyan chief in front of his family, and another large scene shows more than a hundred gods and goddesses and 45 officials greeting the king. There is also a depiction of Pepi II performing the Sed festival. One of the niches still contained a life-sized royal statue, making it the only example to be found in situ in one of these niches.

Three of Pepi II's queens have pyramids. Wedjebten is buried to the south of Pepe II's mortuary complex, while Iput II and Neith are buried to the northwest. A fourth queen, Ankhesenpepi, has a tomb between the pyramids of Iput II and Neith but not a pyramid of her own, suggesting she was considered lower in rank for some reason.

Of the three pyramids, that of Neith is the highest quality. An inscription in her mortuary complex shows she was a daughter of Pepi I and the half-sister of Pepi II, having had a different mother. Brother-sister marriages were not uncommon among the ancient Egyptian royalty. The interior chambers have portions of the Pyramid Texts on the walls, making her the first queen to be so honored.

The causeway leading from Pepi II's mortuary complex runs 400 meters (1,312 ft.) to a now-dry lake. It retains some of its original decoration and shows the king in the guise of a griffin or sphinx defeating his enemies. There are also scenes of people bringing offerings to the dead king, a standard motif. The valley temple has scenes of Pepi II hunting in a swamp, defeating his enemies, and being welcomed by various gods. The layout is typical of these structures, with a long frontage on the water leading to a colonnaded front room plus a few small rooms beyond.

The Middle Kingdom

Pepi II's reign, while long lasting, was not a good one, and there was an increasing shift of power away from the capital at Memphis to the provinces. Local governors called *nomarchs* (after the provinces, or *nomes*, they ruled) built elaborate tombs for themselves in their areas, and when Pepi II died, these *nomarchs* began petty kings. Dynasty VI ended within a few years, as did central rule, ushering in a chaotic time known as the First Intermediate Period (2181-2040 BCE).

During this time, Asiatic people invaded the Nile Delta from the east, and the rulers of Memphis had little power more than a day's march from the city, so the rest of Egypt became a patchwork of warring states whose borders were in constant flux. There is little evidence of activity at Saqqara during this turbulent time – indeed, it is a low point for construction all along the Nile.

The only pyramid built at Saqqara during the First Intermediate Period was during Dynasty VIII for the pharaoh Qakare Ibi (2162?-2161? BCE). While his exact dates are unknown, the

Royal Canon of Turin records that his reign lasted for only 2 years, 1 month, and 1 day. He was based in Memphis and probably did not have control over the entire country. His pyramid at South Saqqara was perhaps an attempt to prove his worth.

Time has not been kind to this pyramid, so only an estimation of its height can be given. It was probably about 21 meters (68.9 ft.) high and 31.5 meters (103.3 ft.) to a side. It perhaps had an angle of 53° 7'. Most of the limestone blocks used for the interior were robbed, but some of the few surviving limestone blocks include a cryptic inscription in red ink mentioning a "chief of the Libyans." It also appears that the outer casing was never completed. Oddly, it was not oriented to the cardinal directions like earlier pyramids but rather on a northwest–southeast axis. The ancient name for this pyramid is unknown.

Despite the damage, the interior is still relatively intact. A corridor leads down from the northwest face past a large granite portcullis to the burial chamber. Both the passageway and burial chamber are inscribed with Pyramid Texts, the last known example of this type of funerary writing. The chamber's roof is flat rather than vaulted and carved with a starry sky.

While the pyramid is in a ruinous state, the mortuary temple on its northeastern face is even more so. It was built of mudbrick, not stone, and has almost completely disappeared. There is no evidence for a causeway or a valley temple. Considering how fragmentary the temple is, if these other features were also built of mudbrick, they might have indeed existed but have since disappeared entirely.

Order was restored during the Middle Kingdom (2040-1782 BCE) by the strong rulers of Dynasty XI, who ruled from Thebes, and since Memphis lost its status as the capital, Saqqara saw little construction as the focus of building projects turned elsewhere. Only a few private tombs have been found at Saqqara dating to this period, and none of them were royal burials.

Just as the Middle Kingdom was ushered in by an age of chaos, it went out with chaos, and that chaotic time is known as the Second Intermediate Period (1782-1570 BCE). Once again, the central government grew weak, although it managed to keep a modicum of authority over both Upper and Lower Egypt. Regional rulers did gain more power, but the period wasn't nearly as troubled as the First Intermediate Period.

Two small pyramids at Saqqara date to this time. They were made of brick and encased in limestone, but they were mostly stripped in antiquity, hastening their deterioration.

The most interesting of these is the pyramid of Khendjer, a Dynasty XIII king who ruled for four years around 1747 BCE. Curiously, Khendjer is an Asiatic name, not an Egyptian one, and it is not known why he had a foreign name. His exact place in the chronology of Dynasty XIII kings also remains unclear; some scholars believe he was the 17th king of the dynasty, while others assert he was the 22nd. This highlights how little is known about the period. It is thought that he ruled from Memphis, hence his burial at South Saqqara.

Khendjer's pyramid once stood 37.35 meters (122.5 ft.) tall and 52.5 meters (172.2 ft.) to a side with an inclination of 55°. The ancient name for this pyramid is unknown, and like many pyramids at Saqqara, its outer casing was taken away, exposing a mudbrick core that has crumbled over the centuries so that it is now one of the most ruined pyramids, standing barely waist high over the surrounding sands. Luckily, the pyramidion, or apex stone of the pyramid, was discovered and shows interesting carvings of the pharaoh making offerings to the gods. The presence of Khendjer on the pyramidion shows that the pyramid was finished in his lifetime, making it the only completed pyramid from this dynasty. Few rulers from this era lasted long enough to even begin the construction of pyramids, let alone finish them.

The interior chambers of this pyramid were preserved because they were dug beneath the base. The entrance is from the west, as is typical of pyramids in this period since it is the direction of the land of the dead. The entrance is blocked by two imposing portcullises made of quartzite, a very hard stone. From there runs a complex network of small passages, and at the center of the pyramid is a burial chamber of quartzite. Despite the hardness of the stone, robbers broke into the tomb and looted it until not a trace of the treasure remained. Only a few fragmentary inscriptions in the vicinity identified this pyramid as being that of Khendjer.

Like many pyramids, Khendjer's had subsidiary tombs. A small pyramid to the northeast had a brick core and three burial shafts. At the bottom of each of these shafts was a burial chamber with a quartzite sarcophagus. It appears that these were intended for the pharaoh's wives, but apparently they were never used. There were also several nearby shaft graves that also appear to have been left empty. The main pyramid is enclosed by a limestone wall, and a second mudbrick wall surrounds the entire mortuary complex.

The mortuary temple on the pyramid's east face has all but vanished. It appears to have been large, but other than some fragments of bas-reliefs and columns, little remains.

An unusual chapel stands on a platform on the north side of the pyramid, accessed by two stairways. There was a false door for the pharaoh's spirit to pass through, but it was placed on the north wall of the chapel, rather than the south wall closest to the pyramid. Why such a departure from convention was done is unknown. A few fragments of carvings from this chapel show offering scenes.

One final pyramid was begun at South Saqqara, most likely in Dynasty XIII. It measured 78.75 meters (258.4 ft.) to a side but never reached its full height. It had the beginnings of a mudbrick core and limestone casing. The substructure was completed, with entrance from the ground a little to the east of the pyramid. Most likely the entrance would have been covered by the mortuary temple, but that temple was never built.

Since no inscription has ever been found associated with this pyramid, it is unknown for whom it was intended, and it is generally called the Southern South Saqqara Pyramid or the Unfinished Pyramid at South Saqqara. Despite its name, however, its substructure was finished and is remarkably complex and extensive, being the largest of any pyramid for that dynasty or the previous one. An entrance on the east side leads to a long staircase down to an alcove where a slot for a portcullis was found, although the portcullis was never installed. This indicates that the burial chamber was never used, since the purpose of the portcullises was to block tomb robbers from entering. The corridor then turns south for a time before turning west again into a room from which two corridors run north. The first dead-ends and was probably intended as a storage chamber. The other descends before turning west and passing two more portcullises before the passage forks to the west and north.

To the west is the burial chamber. Like others of this era, it had a reverse V-shaped ceiling, but this one was never carved with stars. A large hollow quartzite block was intended for housing the sarcophagus, but it was never used.

To the north is a smaller burial chamber containing a sarcophagus lid and a fourth portcullis between the antechamber and vaulted burial chamber. For some reason, the burial chamber comes before the antechamber, something not seen in other pyramids.

While large sections of the mudbrick enclosure wall have been found, no other parts of the mortuary complex appear to have been built.

The New Kingdom and the Apis Cult

After the Second Intermediate Period, Saqqara experienced a renewal of interest during the New Kingdom (1570-1070 BCE), a glorious era of Egyptian history that brought massive building projects all up and down the Nile. Memphis once again became capital for part of the New Kingdom era, and thus Saqqara witnessed more building projects at this time, at least for nobility.

Most royal burials now took place at the Valley of the Kings and Valley of the Queens far up the Nile near Thebes (modern Luxor). Pyramids had gone out of fashion, both because they acted as beacons for tomb robbers and also because they were so expensive. Pharaohs preferred to lavish funds on large temple complexes while excavating tombs for themselves in the rock of the Valley of the Kings. These tombs could also be better hidden from robbers, but except for the tomb of Tutankhamun, all these efforts failed (and even Tutankhamun's tomb was robbed once, although most of the treasure was saved).

Despite this shift of attention to the south, activity continued at Saqqara. The cult of Imhotep remained popular, and many important government figures chose to be buried at Saqqara. A cluster of such tombs are located south of the causeway of the pyramid of Unas. These were in the style of "temple tombs" popular at that time. A small temple on the surface housed the entrance to a vertical shaft leading to the tomb itself. The tombs varied in size, ranging from single chambers to whole networks of rooms and connecting passageways. The walls were lined with carved limestone blocks showing various religious scenes and images of daily life, but sadly most of these were ripped out, either in antiquity to be reused elsewhere or in the 19th century to feed the insatiable demands of collectors.

The most prominent of these was that of the General Horemheb, who ruled as regent for Tutankhamun (1334-1325 BCE) until the boy came of age and later ruled as pharaoh in his own right from 1321-1293 BCE. His tomb at Saqqara is not technically a royal one, which suggests it was started while he was still a regent or perhaps even earlier during his military days. When he ascended the throne as the last ruler of Dynasty XVIII, he built a tomb for himself in the Valley of the Kings, so his Saqqara tomb housed the remains of several members of his family, including perhaps his queen, Mutnodjmet. The tomb is lined with elaborately decorated limestone blocks showing military and religious scenes.

A statue of Horemheb

Next to the tomb of Horemheb is the tomb of Maya, Tutankhamun's treasurer. This, too, has surviving decorations, including a scene that shows Maya and his wife standing before the gods.

On a low rise overlooking Saqqara to the southwest of the pyramid of Teti are more than 30 New Kingdom tomb-chapels cut into the cliff. These were similar in function to the temple-tombs below, in that they had a public temple area blocking off access to the tomb beyond. One such tomb had a well-preserved chapel with extensive decorations and even portions of the sarcophagi and human remains. Another was the tomb of Lady Maia, Tutankhamun's nurse, which has a delightful scene showing the royal child sitting on Maia's lap.

As it turned out, these tombs had been reused in the Late Period to house a large number of mummified cats, so the excavators had to remove thousands of dead cats before they could examine the tombs and their human occupants. Some of the tomb-chapels had been extended and connected with corridors to make a catacomb for the cats.

The most stunning New Kingdom tomb at Saqqara was not for humans, but for bulls. Called the Serapeum, this massive underground catacomb was for the mummified Apis bulls, considered living embodiments of the god Ptah. This deity was one of the main gods of Memphis, the god of craftsmen and architects who brought the whole world into form. The cult of Imhotep considered the famous architect to be Ptah's son, and Ptah was also the patron deity of the Saqqara necropolis.

A statue of the Apis bull found at the Serapeum

As much as the Apis bull was revered by the Egyptians, they esteemed its mother almost equally as much. Although the classical writers wrote far less about the "Mother of the Apis" than the Apis bull, modern archeological work in the Sacred Animal Necropolis of Saqqara has revealed that the bulls' mothers were also given a life of luxury and treated well after their deaths. The account by Strabo mentioned earlier in this book mentions that the Apis' mother had her own sanctuary, but no other details are related. For more details on the Mother of the Apis, modern scholars are forced to turn to archaeology. The earliest known Egyptian reference to the

Mother of the Apis is dated to year thirty-seven of the Twenty-Sixth Dynasty King Amasis (570-526 BCE), or about 534 BCE (Smith et. El. 2011, 4). Although the inscription indicates that Mother of the Apis was a royally recognized sacred animal by the 6th century, the earliest known burial is dated to an early part of the turbulent Twenty-Ninth Dynasty, or sometime between 392 and 388 BCE (Smith et. El. 2011, 4).

Like with the Apis, the Mother of the Apis was mummified and interred in a subterranean catacomb, but its funerary rituals were far less ostentatious. The mother of the Apis bull was not interred in the Serapeum with the bulls, but in a separate section in the Sacred Animal Necropolis.

The cult of the Apis bull played a role in ancient Egyptian religion since the formation of the Egyptian state and the unification of Upper and Lower Egypt, but its popularity continued to increase throughout Pharaonic history. During the New Kingdom, the Apis cult attained a higher status when the Serapeum was built and then expanded under the watchful eyes of Khaemwaset. Still, even during the New Kingdom the Apis cult was primarily the object of only royal patronage; the vast number of Egyptians played little role in the day-to-day functions of the cult. During the Late Period, things began to change dramatically in this regard.

The Apis bulls lived in the temple of Ptah until their death, at which point they achieved immortality and became known as Osiris Apis, after the god who had risen from the dead. The name became shortened to Serapis, hence the name Serapeum. The holy bulls were mummified and buried with full rituals as if they were important human beings.

Picture of a mask for a mummified Apis

Although the Apis cult existed in Egypt by at least the First or Second Dynasty, the burial chambers known as the Serapeum were not built until the New Kingdom (ca. 1550-1075 BCE). More than likely, the Apis bulls were mummified and given official burials proper for a god before the New Kingdom, but currently, the locations of those burials are unknown. Modern archaeologists do know that the Serapeum not only served as the burial chambers for the Apis bulls during the New Kingdom and Late Period, but that the subterranean structure also became a focal point for popular religion. The oldest chambers of the Serapeum were first built during the reign of Amenhotep III (ca. 1388-1351 BCE) of the Eighteenth Dynasty, with work then continuing through the 30th year of Ramesses II (ca. 1279-1213 BCE) of the Nineteenth Dynasty

(Gomaà 1973, 39). The next phase of construction was of the so-called "small chambers," which began during the 21st year of Ramesses II's rule and continued into the reign of the Twenty-Sixth Dynasty King Psamtek I (664-610 BCE). The pharaoh's son Prince Khaemweset oversaw construction of the massive catacomb that can still be visited today. He cut a tunnel with large side chambers to hold the sarcophagi for the bulls, each sarcophagus weighing some 70 tons. These tunnels were expanded under the reign of the Dynasty XXVI pharaoh Psamtik I (664-610 BCE), and during the reign of Nectanebo I (380-362 BCE), a long avenue lined with sphinxes was built leading up to the catacomb.

The final phase in the construction of the Serapeum was the addition of the "great chamber," which Psamtek I started and was subsequently completed by the Ptolemies in the later centuries of the first millennium BCE (Gomaà 1973, 39).

Like all ancient Egyptian mortuary temples, the Serapeum was part of a larger temple complex. The pyramids of the Old and Middle Kingdoms were simply elaborate burial chambers for the deceased kings and served as the focal point of larger temple complexes. In the New Kingdom, large mortuary temples were built where the deceased kings were worshipped, so the Serapeum being part of a larger complex was in line with Egyptian theological traditions. The Apis bull's actual temple was part of an even larger temple complex dedicated to the god Ptah, the god of creation and patron of Memphis, which is where the Apis cult was headquartered.

The section of the Ptah Temple that was dedicated to the Apis bull and its cult was known as the "Per User-Hep" or "House of Osiris-Apis." Located above ground were the temple proper, the bull's living quarters, and the wabet or embalming house (Dimick 1958, 187). The intact embalming table in the embalming house has been dated to the reign of the Twenty-Second Dynasty King Shoshenq I (943-922 BCE) (Jones and Jones 1982, 51), which demonstrates that the kings of Egypt continued to patronize the Apis cult, even during the era of political instability known as the Third Intermediate Period. Based on the reports of the classical authors discussed earlier, and also as the result of modern studies conducted on Egyptian animal mummies, it is believed that the Apis bulls were mummified in essentially the same manner as humans. Due to the size and composition of the bulls, they were mummified on their backs with their stiff legs pointed in the air, which was the only notable difference (Dimick 1958, 188). The internal organs of the bulls were removed and the viscera was placed in four canopic jars. The body was then soaked in natron, wrapped in linen, placed in a cart, and wheeled to its eternal resting place in the Serapeum (Wilkinson 2003, 172).

The interior of the Serapeum is truly impressive. The tunnels are 3 meters (9.8 ft.) wide and 5 meters (16.4 ft.) high and run for almost a kilometer. The chambers housing the massive sarcophagi are at regular intervals on either side of the passageways. Many of the walls are roughly hewn, the strokes from the ancient picks clearly visible. One section has shallow niches that once held plaques, and a few deeper niches all along the passageways would have held lamps. The sarcophagi are polished to a high sheen and many include hieroglyphic inscriptions and false doors for the spirit of the bull to pass through. Only one still retained its bull mummy.

When modern archaeologists first opened the Serapeum in the late 19th century, they not only discovered the mummified remains of many of the bulls but also over 1,000 more or less intact votive stelae (Vandier 1964, 130). Many of the recovered stelae are now housed in the Louvre Museum in Paris where they have been studied for over 100 years by some of the world's top Egyptologists. Most of the inscriptions on the stelae are formulaic in nature and begin with a standard statement that the donor 'provides for the ka' of the Apis (Posener 1936, 41–46). Perhaps the most important information gleaned from Serapeum votive stelae are the backgrounds of the donors. The nobles are included among the numbers of the donors, but along with them are peasants, artisans, merchants, and soldiers (Sadek 1988, 271). The Apis cult was open to all Egyptians to participate in during the 1st millennium BCE.

Obviously, there are too many votive stelae from the Serapeum to even reprint some of their content, but one, in particular, relates in detail what the average person wanted the Apis bull to know. The stela in question was donated by a general named Ahmose, who served in the Egyptian army under the last king of the Twenty-Sixth Dynasty and under the Persians of the Twenty-Seventh Dynasty since the piece has been dated to that period. The text states, "Apis-Osiris, the revered one, who is near the unique friend, the general Ahmose, son of Pasabar, born of Takapenakhbit. He said concerning the bringing of this god in peace to the Beautiful West after his making every ceremony in the embalming room, bringing him in his radiance of the chief of archers, controller of foreign troops and the elite army troops until reaching this god at its place in the necropolis. 'I am the servant who provides for your ka every day guarding at night, not sleeping, searching all of your excellent things, meanwhile, your respect is in the hearts of everyone and the foreigners of all foreign lands who are upon Egypt. That which is made in your embalming room by me as well as sending a message to the south, moreover to the north straightaway and all the mayors of the cities and districts shall come moreover, bringing it to your embalming room.' Now the prophet of the gods of the temple of Ptah said, 'Oh Apis-Osiris, you hear the worship of that which is of your glory (by) the general Ahmose. He made mourning on your back, he came himself under silver and gold of the royal unguent and every precious stone and every good thing. You shall make reward like that which he makes for you passing his years, you shall (make) stable his name eternally and one shall establish this stela in the necropolis of the beloved, remembering his name forever.'" (Posener 1936). Besides the name and titles, the text of Ahmose's votive stela is similar to the others recovered from the Serapeum.

A stela dedicated to the Apis dating to the 7th century BCE

Along with the stelae, Egyptians could also donate other items to be placed in the burial chambers, depending, of course, on the person's financial status. Essentially, the logic behind donating items to the deceased Apis bulls was the same as one would do for a deceased person, as the items donated were believed to have been available in the afterlife. Thus, since Ahmose was a high-ranking officer in the army, he was able to donate more expensive items in addition to the votive stela. The average Egyptian was able to more actively participate in the cult of the Apis bull during the Late Period, but the importance of the cult was not lost on the rulers during the period.

The view that the ancient Greeks took toward Egypt can best be described as paternalistic. They were impressed with Egypt's antiquity and even believed that many aspects of their own culture originated in Egypt, but they still believed that Hellenic culture was superior. The

Ptolemies, who were the Greek rulers of Egypt after Alexander's conquest, believed in the idea of Greek cultural superiority, often called "Hellenism," and promoted it in the new Greek city of Alexandria. With that said, the Greek rulers of Egypt did not entirely abandon all aspects of Pharaonic culture, which included the Apis cult. The 1st century CE Greek historian Arrian reported in his account of Alexander's conquests that one of the first stops the legendary general made in Egypt was to the Ptah Temple in Memphis. "From Heliopolis he crossed the river to Memphis, where, among the other gods, he offered a special sacrifice to Apis and held Games with both athletic and literary contests… He proceeded around Lake Mareotis and finally came ashore at the spot where Alexandria, the city which bears his name, now stands." (Arrian, The Conquests of Alexander, III, 1–2). Although Alexander recognized the importance of the Apis cult to the Egyptians, his visit was for the most part obligatory. It also shows that the Greeks were willing to change and adapt the Apis cult to accommodate their own cultural background.

Thousands of years later, the Serapeum is still somewhat mysterious. There are only 24 sarcophagi, far too few if every Apis bull was buried with full honors as the texts say they were. Did the cult of Ptah only bury some bulls? Did they reuse the sarcophagi? Are there other massive bull catacombs lying hidden in the sands awaiting discovery? The few inscriptions in the Serapeum do not clarify the issue, but they do give some interesting insights. When the Persian king Cambyses II (ruled Egypt 525-522 BCE) occupied Egypt, he performed a number of outrages against the native religion, including stabbing an Apis bull to death. An inscription in the Serapeum proudly records the burial of a bull with the full ceremony in 523 BCE, demonstrating that the Egyptians would not be intimidated by the tyrant.

The Late Period and the Greco-Roman Period

After the New Kingdom, Egypt fell into another period of unrest called the Third Intermediate Period (1069-525 BCE), followed by a brief resurgence in the Late Period (525-332 BCE) before becoming a Greek kingdom and then a Roman colony. Saqqara continued to be an important site, and it was during the often-overlooked Late Period that the site acquired one of its most interesting and unusual features.

In the northern edge of the site are a number of catacombs filled with literally millions of animal mummies. Egyptian gods and goddesses each had their particular sacred animal, and their temples often had collections of these animals that were well cared for as living manifestations of the divine. A sacrifice of one of these animals, carefully mummified and buried with certain rituals in a sanctified space, brought the donor's prayers to the gods. This practice had been ongoing for centuries but was especially popular in the Late Period at Saqqara and numerous other sites all along the Nile.

The majority of animal mummies at North Saqqara are ibises. The mummified ibises were wrapped in linen and coated with resin before being stored in large, undecorated, tapering jars. These pots were placed in modified Old Kingdom mastabas that had been cleared of their previous residents and connected with tunnels in order to create a series of catacombs. Cows were buried at the tops of the vertical shafts and also between the mastabas as part of a ritual to sanctify the area.

Ibises were sacred to Thoth, the god of writing, learning, and wisdom, and it is interesting to note that the deified Imhotep also had these traits and the two cults shared a close relationship. This has led some Egyptologists to speculate that Imhotep's tomb may be somewhere in the vicinity.

Another tomb had a row of niches, each containing a mummified baboon encased in a wooden shrine. Baboons were a symbol of a couple of gods, including Babi and Thoth, and it is the latter deity who was most likely being honored here. Baboons were rare imports from south of the Sahara, but ibises are native to Egypt, so it is not surprising that the ibises far outnumber the baboons.

Connected with the baboon catacomb is another for falcons and hawks, which were sacred to Horus, who had a number of different aspects including being the protector of the pharaoh. Nearby was a large underground complex similar to the Serapeum called the Mothers of Apis. It was here that the cows that gave birth to the Apis Bulls were interred. Each cow was placed in a stone sarcophagus in a large arched vault lined with limestone blocks.

Experts who analyzed the bird mummies revealed a few surprises. While from the outside they had the shape of an entire animal, a large portion of the bird mummies were incomplete. Some wrappings contain only a bone or feather of the bird, while some have a different species of bird than the one represented by the shape of the mummy. For example, some falcon mummies actually contain just a few parts of an ibis. Since the ibis was a much more common bird, was this evidence of the priests fooling the public? Egyptologists are divided on this, and while some believe that it is a sign of cheating, others assert that a portion of the animal could be a stand in for the entire animal, although probably a cheaper option for poorer worshippers. This practice has been found at other sites as well - in one study by Manchester University, about a third of a large sample of animal mummies contained no animal parts.

There is some textual evidence for cheating. A collection of ostraca (fragments of pottery that have been written on) found in North Saqqara constitute an archive for a priest named Hor who wrote around 172-162 BCE. It explains how the priests had a rule that only one animal should go in each pot, but this hadn't been followed and often the pots were stuffed with as many mummies as would fit, presumably to save money. Thus, Hor complains that the faithful weren't getting the complete service.

A couple of sections of one of the ibis catacombs were filled with birds that had not been put into pots, and this may have been a further example of cheating on the part of the priests or perhaps a cheaper option for prayers, or maybe even a full and accepted ritual at one period of time. Despite the wealth of textual data surviving from ancient Egypt, there are still many unanswered questions about their culture.

Another depository for animal mummies is the so-called dog catacomb. This underground structure near the temple to Anubis, the jackal-headed god of cemeteries and embalming, was first discovered in the 1890s by French Egyptologist Jacques De Morgan. In 2011, further excavations by a British and Egyptian team uncovered an estimated 8 million animal mummies, about half of them birds but also a large number of dogs and some cats and mongooses. The dogs come from several different breeds, and the majority of them were newborns. Analysis of the bones suggests the dogs had been specially bred, most likely for the purposes of being sacrificed.

Excavations of these animal catacombs are ongoing, and unlike the Serapeum, they are not open to the public because of the continuing work and the unstable nature of many of the catacombs.

Numerous human burials at Saqqara also date to the Late Period. A French team discovered a major collection of them in 2006 and subsequent years in an area north of the Unas Causeway. Many were simple burials in the sand, while others were vertical shafts leading down to one or two small chambers. Some of these were reused Old Kingdom tombs, but others were built in the Late Period. The burials in the sand have few grave goods and are situated between the rock-hewn tombs.

The superstructures on these tombs varied. Some had modest stone buildings or surrounding walls, while three had mudbrick pyramids only a few meters tall. These miniature pyramids were popular in the Late and Greco-Roman periods.

The shafts contained multiple burials and had numerous wooden mummy cases, painted plaster cartonnages, and mummies without cases stacked in neat piles filling the small chambers leading off from the shafts. One cartonnage, with an inscription saying it belonged to the lady Nephthys-iyti, is covered in gold leaf. Other grave goods included baskets with food offerings, ceramics, statuettes of various deities, and magical amulets. Some papyrus fragments included the Egyptian demotic script from the 5th-3rd centuries BCE and some Aramaic writing from the 5th century BCE. These finds are especially significant because it is rare to come across undisturbed tombs. Work is ongoing on these tombs, and it is possible the site still has some surprises in store.

During the Greco-Roman Period, Saqqara continued to be a popular site for animal mummies and general worship. One interesting construction from the Ptolemaic period that still stands today is the so-called "Philosophers circle", a half-circle of statues portraying important Greek thinkers and poets, including Hesiod, Homer, Pindar, Plato, and others. While fragmentary, these Greek statues, within sight of Egypt's earliest pyramid, indicate just how long activity went on at Saqqara.

In fact, Saqqara remained a holy site long after the ancient religions had disappeared. Several Coptic monasteries were built there in the early Middle Ages, and some of these Christian houses of worship continued to operate even after the Islamic conquest in 642. This makes Saqqara one of the oldest continuously used holy sites in the world.

Online Resources

Other books about Egypt by Charles River Editors

Other books about ancient history by Charles River Editors

Other books about Saqqara on Amazon

Bibliography

Baines, John and Jaromír Málek. *Atlas of Ancient Egypt.* New York City, NY: Facts on File, Inc., 1985.

Bárta, Miroslav, Filip Coppens, and Jaromir Krejčí (editors). *Abusir and Saqqara in the Year 2010/1.* Prague, Czech Republic: Czech Institute of Egyptology, Faculty of Arts, Charles University in Prague, 2011.

Clayton, Peter A. *The Complete Pharaohs: The Reign-by-Reign Record of the Rulers and Dynasties of Ancient Egypt.* Cairo, Egypt: The American University in Cairo Press, 2006.

Dodson, Aidan. *After the Pyramids: The Valley of the Kings and Beyond.* London, United Kingdom: The Rubicon Press, 2000.

Dodson, Aidan. "The tombs of Tutankhamun's people: Seeking Saqqara's New Kingdom tombs" in *Current World Archaeology* 36, July 2009.

Grimal, Nicolas. *A History of Ancient Egypt.* Oxford, United Kingdom: Blackwell Publishers, 1992.

Lehner, Mark. *The Complete Pyramids: Solving the Ancient Mysteries.* New York City, New York: Thames & Hudson, 1997.

Nicolson, Paul T. "Cult, caches, and catacombs: The animal necropolis" in *Current World Archaeology* 36, July 2009.

Wilkinson, Richard H. *The Complete Temples of Ancient Egypt.* New York City, New York: Thames & Hudson, 2000.

Wilkinson, Richard H. *The Complete Gods and Goddesses of Ancient Egypt.* Cairo, Egypt: The

American University in Cairo Press, 2005.

Free Books by Charles River Editors

We have brand new titles available for free most days of the week. To see which of our titles are currently free, click on this link.

Discounted Books by Charles River Editors

We have titles at a discount price of just 99 cents everyday. To see which of our titles are currently 99 cents, click on this link.

Printed in Great Britain
by Amazon